Women as Terrorists

Women as Terrorists

Mothers, Recruiters, and Martyrs

R. Kim Cragin and Sara A. Daly

PRAEGER SECURITY INTERNATIONAL
An Imprint of ABC-CLIO, LLC

A B C ⬢ C L I O

Santa Barbara, California • Denver, Colorado • Oxford, England

Library of Congress Cataloging-in-Publication Data
Cragin, Kim.
  Women as terrorists : mothers, recruiters, and martyrs /
R. Kim Cragin and Sara A. Daly.
      p. cm.
  Includes bibliographical references and index.
  ISBN 978-0-275-98909-5 (hardcopy : alk. paper) — ISBN 978-0-313-05944-5 (ebook)
  1. Women terrorists. I. Daly, Sara A. II. Title.
  HV6431.C734   2009
  363.325082—dc22   2009006252

13 12 11 10 9   1 2 3 4 5

This book is also available on the World Wide Web as an eBook.
Visit www.abc-clio.com for details.

ABC-CLIO, LLC
130 Cremona Drive, P.O. Box 1911
Santa Barbara, California 93116–1911

This book is printed on acid-free paper ∞

Manufactured in the United States of America

Contents

Preface

In the months following the 11 September 2001 attacks by al-Qa'ida on New York City's World Trade Center and the Pentagon building in Virginia, two women counterterrorism experts became friends. These women each brought a unique background and experience to the friendship: one had spent significant time "in the field" as an academic researcher, particularly in the Middle East and Southeast Asia; the other had an extensive background in the U.S. government, and specifically the intelligence community, on counterterrorism issues. And so, through this friendship, these women began to challenge each other in their own work and daily lives. While some might view this friendship as unremarkable, women still do not have a strong presence in the U.S. academic or policy-making community on national security issues. To be honest, those women who are involved in national security tend to view each other suspiciously and competitively, rather than cooperatively. So it is fair to say that the friendship forged by these two women was both unique and remarkable.

This book, in many ways, is a product of that friendship. *Women as Terrorists* addresses the topic of women terrorists through the eyes of women counterterrorism experts. In the various chapters, readers will note both the horror and sympathy that we feel toward the victims of terrorist attacks. Indeed, one of the abiding characteristics of terrorism is that it affects a much wider collection of individuals than the attacks' immediate victims. Having researched terrorism for many years, we cannot help but be affected by the tragedies experienced again and again by innocent people at the hands of terrorists and terrorist groups. Nevertheless, readers also will note a certain degree of empathy that we found for our research subjects as *women* who continuously attempted to find their place in the midst of male-dominated terrorist groups and even wider societal revolutions. In this sense, this book should be of interest to individuals—men and women who empathize with women's struggle for equality—because the women terrorists in this book clearly worked and fought to be taken seriously by terrorist leaders and within their wider communities. Of course, one cannot set aside the fact that these women actively sought the death of innocent civilians. And so, this book also should be of interest to those studying terrorism, especially those searching for new ways to gain insight into the internal dynamics of terrorist groups. Indeed, we would argue that although the topic of women as terrorists contains an inherent interest in and of itself, by looking at how terrorist leaders choose to deploy women, we can better understand terrorist decision making and the internal workings of terrorist groups themselves. Similarly, this book should be of interest to those who want to understand the motivations of terrorists: how and why people come to believe that violence against innocent civilians is a credible pathway. In looking at women as terrorists, the chapters tell myriad stories about the lives, thoughts, and feelings of these women. As such, it provides insight into terrorist motivations and perhaps even how the motivations of women terrorists differ from those of men.

Women as Terrorists, therefore, addresses the roles that women have played in a wide variety of terrorist groups and over a period of approximately thirty years. A basic summary of these terrorist groups appears in Chapter 1, "Terrorist Motivations and Group Dynamics." For example, the book discusses how terrorist groups with religious objectives, such as al-Qa'ida and Lebanese Hizballah, have incorporated women into their overarching strategy and worldview. Al-Qa'ida, in particular, has struggled to contextualize the demand placed upon it by Muslim women with its socially conservative worldview. This tension manifested itself in December 2007 and January 2008, when women responded to an offer by Ayman al-Zawahiri, al-Qa'ida's second in command, to ask him questions via an al-Qa'ida Web site. Many of these questions related to the roles that women could play in al-Qa'ida, and it was clear that his conservative answers were less than satisfactory. Although it is arguable that al-Qa'ida faces many dilemmas in the practical application of its worldview—for example, many have commented that al-Qa'ida leaders do not seem to know how an Islamic Caliphate might be governed—the role of women in the al-Qa'ida movement reveals some unique and fascinating tensions.

In this book, we also examine more rural-based guerrilla movements, such as Sendero Luminoso or the Shining Path in Peru. Led by Abimael Guzmán, who was a professor at a rural university in that country, Sendero Luminoso utilized women extensively and in a wide variety of roles, from recruiter to guerrilla fighter. In the lore of the Shining Path, moreover, women have been touted as more dedicated and even more violent than their male counterparts. Truth or fiction, this perception of Shining Path women presents an interesting contrast with the women members and sympathizers of al-Qa'ida. Finally, this book includes a discussion of women terrorists involved in left-wing, western European groups, such as the Baader-Meinhof Gang or the Provisional Irish Republican Army, which conducted terrorist attacks in the 1960s, 1970s, 1980s, and even 1990s. The women in these western European terrorist groups often framed and interpreted their participation through the lens of women's equality. That is, the struggle for equality often was viewed by women members of western European terrorist groups as part of a wider nationalist, leftist, or separatist agenda. We attempt to discover and explain why women became involved in terrorist groups, how terrorist leaders deliberated and eventually utilized women to achieve their objectives, and how women's presence in turn affected the recruitment of new fighters and supporters into the terrorist movement.

To do this, the book is structured around the various roles that women have played in terrorist groups, rather than around the terrorist groups themselves. We find this approach somewhat more interesting and insightful than typical case study analyses, because it allows a way to compare and contrast the women involved in many varied terrorist and insurgent groups. In each of these chapters we also attempt to provide to our readers examples of women who have chosen to join terrorist and insurgent groups and their thoughts and feelings about this choice, as well as how terrorist leaders utilized women to achieve their political objectives.

Chapter 1, "Terrorist Motivations and Group Dynamics," begins with a discussion of how experts have traditionally understood the terrorism phenomenon in general and how this understanding has evolved over time. Chapter 1 argues that it is useful to examine terrorists as organizational entities that put time and resources into sustaining themselves and reaching out to wider support communities. While the role of women might be muted in some respects with regards to terrorist attacks, women tend to play a more significant role in sustaining the terrorist group and helping terrorist leaders reach out to wider support communities. Additionally, Chapter 1 argues that individuals— men and women—do not just wake up one morning and decide to become a terrorist. Rather, individuals experience a number of factors that move them through a radicalization process. Women might experience some factors differently than men, but they still exhibit patterns of radicalization.

Chapter 2, "Women as Logisticians," suggests that women have typically played the role of logistician in terrorist groups. A logistician might courier money and weapons to various terrorist cells or guerrilla fighters. For example, terrorist leaders have asked women members to conceal messages or explosive devices and smuggle them past security officials. Women also might establish and maintain safe havens for terrorist groups. Of the twenty-two terrorist and insurgent groups that we examine in this book, all but one of them used women as logisticians. While one might assume that logisticians risk little, as compared to operatives or guerrilla fighters, security officials often target the logistical networks of terrorist groups, and so women logisticians have been imprisoned for their activities.

Chapter 3, "Women as Recruiters," explores a role not often addressed in other studies of women terrorists, or indeed, terrorism in general. Yet recruiters play an important role in most terrorist groups: seeking out new members and even filtering through grassroots volunteers. In some instances, terrorist leaders have asked women to help gather new recruits, through family ties or their relationships with students. These new recruits are sometimes women, but often they turn out to be male colleagues in the terrorist group itself. Alternatively, women sometimes have taken on the role of recruiter without direction or guidance from terrorist leaders. Of the twenty-two terrorist and insurgent groups that we explored for this study, seven used women specifically to recruit new members.

Chapter 4, "Women as Suicide Bombers," addresses the somewhat controversial topic of women suicide bombers. To do this, the chapter is divided into two sections: motivations and deployment. That is, the chapter attempts to explore the motivations of female suicide bombers based on their own testimonials and that of their families. Of the twenty-two terrorist and insurgent groups in our study, eight have used women as suicide bombers, exceeding that of recruiters, but not by much. In Chapter 4 we also compare the motivations of female suicide bombers to that of their male counterparts. Beyond motivations, however, this chapter explores the attitudes of terrorist leaders toward female suicide bombers, including the operational advantages and moral disadvantages that they present to terrorist leaders. This dilemma faced by terrorist leaders is particularly interesting and is not fully explored by other studies.

Chapter 5, "Women as Operational Leaders and Fighters," focuses on how different terrorist groups have used women as fighters—either guerrilla fighters or operational leaders—to forward their political, economic, or social objectives. In many instances, a woman might enter a particular terrorist group as a logistician and work her way up to be an operational leader, or, alternatively, a woman could become a senior official responsible for a terrorist group's finances, but never carry or shoot a gun. Of the twenty-two groups in our study, thirteen saw the emergence of female operational leaders or guerrilla fighters.

Significantly, the women in our study who fought side by side with their male counterparts often expressed feminist objectives in correlation with the political objectives espoused by the terrorist group itself. This correlation did not occur with the female suicide bombers in our study. Unlike with male operatives, female guerrilla fighters and female suicide bombers evidence some important motivational differences.

Chapter 6, "Women as Political Vanguards," focuses on how some women have adopted the role of strategic thinkers in the central committees or senior leadership of terrorist groups, as well as their associated wider political, social, and economic movements. This chapter also explores the various symbolic roles that women have played, galvanizing support and multiplying the immediate impact of a specific terrorist attack. Finally, Chapter 6 examines some women who have run for political office and yet represented political parties associated with terrorist groups. Of the twenty-two different terrorist and insurgent groups in this book, twelve witnessed women in the role of vanguards.

Chapter 7, "Women as Terrorists: Past, Present, and Future," provides our basic findings and conclusions from this book. In this chapter, we discuss five overarching findings. First, terrorist leaders think about a female cadré differently than their male counterparts. That is, when terrorist leaders deploy women, they have to weigh the potential backlash in community support against the operational benefit that women might bring, especially in socially conservative societies. Second, female terrorists, like women everywhere, have fought for the right to play a significant role in terrorist groups. Sometimes they are able to achieve prominence in their respective groups, but often women terrorists have expressed frustration at the fact that they are treated with less respect by their male counterparts. Third, terrorist and insurgent groups that have incorporated women into their operations have been able to expand their capabilities and success. Fourth, in the terrorism and counterterrorism expert communities, the role that women have played behind the scenes has been largely discounted, and yet, fifth, behind-the-scenes activities can be essential for the terrorist group in order to sustain its violent activities, as well as its wider support base and so should not be dismissed. In conclusion, Chapter 7 also attempts to look into the future and identify new ways that terrorist groups might attempt to utilize women.

ACKNOWLEDGMENTS

Of course, this book would not have been possible without the forbearance shown by our families, particularly our husbands, as we took time out of our nights and weekends to conduct the research and write the chapters. We undertook to write this book perhaps without understanding the amount of time or effort it would eventually demand. Nonetheless, the research itself was rewarding and so we thank our families for their enthusiastic support. Special thanks to Nate Shestak for his help with research on Iraqi suicide bombers. Robert Hutchinson, at Praeger, also patiently extended deadlines and provided feedback to two authors reaching beyond their normal readership—terrorism experts—to a wider audience. Nevertheless, we expect some mistakes will be found in this book and, if so, they are our responsibility alone.

Abbreviations

AQI	al-Qa'ida in Iraq
ETA	Euskadi Ta Askatasuna
EZLN	Ejército Zapatista de Liberación Nacional (Zapatistas)
FARC	Fuerzas Armadas Revolucionarias de Colombia (Revolutionary Armed Forces of Colombia)
GIA	Groupe Islamique Arme
Hamas	Harakat al-Muqawama al-Islamiyya
JI	Jemaah Islamiyya
JRA	Japanese Red Army
LTTE	Liberation Tigers of Tamil Eelam
PFLP	Popular Front for the Liberation of Palestine
PIJ	Palestinian Islamic Jihad
PIRA	Provisional Irish Republican Army
PKK	Partiya Karkerên Kurdistan (Kurdish Workers' Party)
PLO	Palestine Liberation Organization
RAF	Red Army Faction or Baader-Meinhof Gang
RB	Red Brigades

1

Terrorist Motivations and Group Dynamics

There is something disturbing about the concept of women as terrorists. Perhaps it has to do with the feminine identity as nurturer—women are mothers, sisters, and wives, but not killers. So it is shocking to witness on television a mother extolling the death of her son, happy that he became a suicide bomber. Nevertheless, mothers *have praised* their sons' sacrifices in villages as distant and dissimilar as Khan Younis in the Palestinian Gaza Strip and Thopigala in Sri Lanka.

In the same way, it is also shocking to learn that female operatives played a significant role in the Beslan school hostage crisis, which occurred on 1 September 2004 in the North Caucasus. Thirty-two Chechen separatists, including two women, took approximately 1,300 people hostage at that time and demanded that Russia give Chechnya formal independence. The women reportedly wore suicide explosive belts, and one threatened to kill anyone who hid a mobile phone, plus three others, for retribution. After Russian forces raided the school, it was determined that 334 people had been killed as part of the hostage crisis, including 184 children, which made it one of the most deadly events in the history of terrorism.

Indeed, one of the most high-profile political assassinations in modern history also occurred at the hands of a female terrorist. On 21 May 1991, former Prime Minister of India Rajiv Gandhi was assassinated by a suicide bomber in Tamil Nadu, India. Gandhi had been campaigning for the Congress Party and left his motorcade to walk along the road and greet his supporters. A woman approached him with a wreath, handed Gandhi the gift, bent down to touch his feet in respect, and then detonated a suicide belt hidden beneath her clothes. Chilling!

Counterterrorism officials have admitted that they too are disturbed by the thought of women as terrorists. In her book, *Shoot the Women First*, Eileen MacDonald recounted that Interpol had advised European counterterrorism units to prioritize the female terrorists of leftist revolutionary cells.[1] According to MacDonald, this prioritization appeared to be the result of two very different reasons: some officials felt that women were more determined and so should be shot first, while other officials felt that they needed to compensate for reluctance in counterterrorism units to shoot a female terrorist. Either explanation suggests some visceral negative reaction in the minds of male security officials at the concept of women as terrorists.

As counterterrorism researchers, we have witnessed the same reaction in the security officials whom we have interviewed. For example, in one breath a hardened Singhalese military officer brazenly told of beheading a male terrorist operative, but subsequently cringed when he recounted watching a female terrorist unit all swallow potassium cyanide capsules as his forces surrounded and then attempted to capture them. It is a story that certainly suggests a high degree of determination on the part of female terrorists in Sri Lanka, at the very least, but it also demonstrates how even hardened counterterrorism and counterinsurgency officers struggle with the concept of women as terrorists.

Perhaps that is why women continue to be part of terrorist groups: they are effective. Women appear less suspicious and so can better slip past guards, more easily hide suicide explosive belts, and use their "feminine wiles" on unsuspecting security officials.[2] Nevertheless, effectiveness is unlikely to be the full explanation for the presence of women in terrorist groups, and effectiveness also is unlikely to be the full explanation for the different operational roles that women have assumed in terrorist organizations. This book, therefore, explores the roles that women have played in terrorist organizations around the world. The purpose of the stories told in this book is not so much to determine whether or not women actually play *significant* roles in terrorist groups. Nor is the purpose of the book to argue that women are necessarily motivated any differently than men. Rather, we simply find the topic interesting and believe that by looking at terrorist groups through the lens of women, one can learn more about the phenomenon itself.

To do this, we examine a variety of different terrorist groups, focusing primarily on the following:

Al-Aqsa Martyrs' Brigades. This terrorist group is a militant offshoot of the Palestinian organization Fatah. It articulates primarily a Palestinian nationalist agenda, although its rhetoric sometimes borrows from its Islamist competitor, Hamas. Al-Aqsa Martyrs' Brigades rose to prominence during the al-Aqsa Intifada, which began in September 2000 and continued until Palestinians agreed to a ceasefire (*hudna*) with Israel in June 2003. The al-Aqsa Martyrs' Brigades sponsored the most female suicide bombers in the Palestinian territories during the al-Aqsa Intifada.

Al-Qa'ida. This terrorist group emerged out of the Soviet–Afghanistan war in the mid-1980s, but since has established branches in multiple countries, including Afghanistan, Iraq (al-Qa'ida in Iraq, or AQI), Saudi Arabia (al-Qa'ida in the Arabian Peninsula), Yemen (Islamic Army of Aden-Abyan), Lebanon (Fatah al-Islam), Indonesia (Jemaah Islamiyya, or JI), the Philippines (Abu Sayyaf Group), and North Africa (al-Qa'ida in the Islamic Maghreb). Al-Qa'ida was responsible for the September 2001 attacks against the World Trade Center and the Pentagon. Although AQI has sponsored women suicide bombers, women have not played a significant role in al-Qa'ida as operatives beyond Iraq. Nevertheless, women have acted as logisticians and recruiters in many of these locations around the world.

Chechen Separatists. These individuals fight for independence from Russia. Ethnically divergent from Russians, Chechens are also Muslim and have had connections, periodically, with al-Qa'ida. Most of these connections, however, occurred during the Soviet–Afghanistan war in the mid-1980s. The Russian and foreign media have come to call the female Chechen rebels, most of whom have become suicide bombers, the Black Widows.

Euskadi Ta Askatasuna (ETA). This militant group operates primarily in Spain. It began in the late 1950s as a Basque nationalist movement with a Marxist–Leninist ideology. ETA members were associated closely with the Provisional Irish Republican Army (PIRA) and the Palestine Liberation Organization (PLO) during the 1970s and 1980s, even participating in joint training activities. Women mostly have played a supporting role in ETA, but Maria Soledad Iparraguirre Guenechea apparently took command of ETA in September 2000.

Groupe Islamique Arme (GIA). This militant group emerged in the early 1990s in response to a decision by the Algerian government to declare void the electoral victory of the Islamic Salvation Front. The primary objective of the GIA is to establish an Islamic government in Algeria. This militant group is well known for is massacres of opponents in Algeria as well as its efforts to attack expatriates living in that country. The GIA also has historical ties to al-Qa'ida.

Harakat al-Muqawama al-Islamiyya (Hamas). This militant group operates in the West Bank and Gaza Strip. Founded in the late 1980s during the first Palestinian Intifada, Hamas fights for an Islamic Palestinian state. As part of this fight, Hamas members have conducted a number of suicide bombings against civilians in Israel. Interestingly, Hamas members also won a majority representation in the Palestinian Legislative Elections in January 2006; five of the Hamas victors were women. Women play a supporting role in Hamas's militant activities, more than an operational role, although the organization reportedly has sponsored a select few female suicide bombers.

Hizballah. This militant group is based primarily in Lebanon. Created in the early 1980s, Hizballah was one of a series of Shi'ite militias that fought against the presence of U.S., European, and Israeli security forces in that country. After a vicious civil war in the 1980s, Saudi Arabia, Syria, and Iran brokered a peace deal in the 1989 Taif Accords, in which Christian and Shi'ite militias were forced to give up their weapons. Hizballah was the exception: it was allowed to keep its weapons as long as it only used violence against Israeli security forces occupying southern Lebanon. Israeli forces eventually withdrew from Lebanon in May 2000, but even since that time, especially in the summer of 2006, Hizballah and Israel have continued their mutual aggression. Women have not engaged in militant activities for Hizballah, but have taken on the roles of logistician, recruiter, and political vanguard.

Jemaah Islamiyya (JI). This militant group operates primarily in Southeast Asia. It was responsible for the October 2002 attack against tourists in Bali that killed more than 200 people, as well as subsequent attacks on the Australian Embassy and Marriott Hotel in Jakarta. One of the key operational leaders for JI, "Hambali," had historical ties to al-Qa'ida senior leadership. He was arrested by Thai authorities in August 2003.

Japanese Red Army (JRA). Fusako Shigenobu established the JRA in the early 1970s. Its stated objective was to overthrow the Japanese government, but it also attempted to aid the Palestinian terrorist groups in their struggle against Israel. Most experts believed that the JRA only had between forty and fifty members, even at its greatest strength. Nonetheless, its members occupied the French Embassy in the Netherlands in 1974 and held its ambassador hostage until negotiations obtained his release. Shigenobu was arrested by Japanese authorities in November 2000, after she returned to the country from her exile in Lebanon.

Liberation Tigers of Tamil Eelam (LTTE). This militant group fights in Sri Lanka to establish an independent state for Tamils. A highly innovative group, the LTTE has an elite suicide-bombing unit called the Black Tigers, and as of July 2006, the Black Tigers had 199 male and 74 female martyrs. The LTTE also has its own female brigade called the Birds of Freedom.

Partiya Karkerên Kurdistan (PKK). Founded in the 1970s, this militant group operates in Turkey, has ties to the Kurdish region in Iraq, and is also known as the Kurdish Workers' Party. It wants to establish an independent Kurdish country that incorporates territory from Turkey, Iraq, Syria, and Iran. As part of this fight, Kurdish women have played both operational and supporting roles for the PKK and are well known for their suicide missions.

Palestinian Islamic Jihad (PIJ). This militant group operates primarily in the West Bank and Gaza Strip. It was established by Fathi Shaqaqi, who was subsequently assassinated by Israeli security authorities. PIJ wants to establish an Islamic state in the Palestinian Territories. Unlike Hamas, however, PIJ has rejected the electoral process in the West Bank and Gaza Strip.

Popular Front for the Liberation of Palestine (PFLP). This militant group was founded in the late 1960s and generally was considered the second largest Palestinian terrorist group after Fatah in the 1970s and 1980s. It conducted a series of airline hijackings during this period, including an El Al flight from Tel Aviv to Rome that reportedly had then-Israeli General Rabin as a passenger. Although the PFLP is considered part of the PLO, it has competed against Fatah on and off for recruits and credibility, even running its own candidates in the Palestinian national elections in the mid-1990s.

Prima Linea. Founded in the 1970s, Prima Linea (or Front Line) conducted its first attacks in 1976, including the assassination of a government official, Enrico Pedenovi. This leftist group was a splinter off of the Red Brigades (RB) in Italy. Most of its members were drawn from Italy's youth movement and, as such, they specifically articulated a feminist agenda that often dictated its target selection. The ideological basis of the Prima Linea also included anarchist components. Although it attempted to advocate for the masses, Prima Linea never had a strong mass following, and most members had dissociated themselves from the group by the early 1980s.

Provisional Irish Republican Army (PIRA). This militant group fought against British rule in Northern Ireland. Its political wing, Sinn Fein, negotiated with the U.K. government as part of the 1998 Good Friday Accords. Members of the PIRA tended to call in the location of bombs so that civilians could evacuate to the extent possible, and they never conducted suicide attacks. Although women never played a central leadership role in the PIRA, they nevertheless have been involved in the planning and execution of attacks as well as in support roles.

Red Army Faction (RAF). Also known as the Baader-Meinhof Gang, this terrorist group was founded in the late 1960s and articulated a communist agenda. With historical and membership roots in Germany's youth movement, this group is particularly interesting because a number of the founding members were women.

Red Brigades (RB). This Italian militant group operated in the 1970s and 1980s. It was a Marxist–Leninist group that was founded to create a communist government in Italy. Most of the members had originally been part of the Communist Youth Movement, and its supporters were drawn from factories and unions. The RB was founded by Alberto Franceschini, Rento Curio, and his girlfriend (to be wife) Mara Cogal.

Fuerzas Armadas Revolucionarias de Colombia (Revolutionary Armed Forces of Colombia FARC). This militant group operates primarily in rural southwest Colombia. Founded in the mid-1960s, the FARC group purports to establish a Marxist revolution in Colombia, although it is also heavily involved in drug trafficking. FARC has approximately 12,000 members of which 30 percent are women. Several FARC units are commanded by women.

Sendero Luminoso. Sendero Luminoso (or the Shining Path) operated in Peru during the 1960s, 1970s, 1980s, and 1990s. Abiemael Guzmán founded the Shining Path in Ayacucho, a rural district in southeastern Peru. He was a university professor and utilized his teacher–student relationship with some of the women to persuade them to recruit for his causes. The Shining Path was particularly brutal in the 1990s and threatened Peru itself. Women fought with their male comrades, and some became well known for their skills in operational planning and ruthlessness.

Sandinista National Liberation Front. The Sandinistas were a revolutionary movement whose primary objective was the overthrow of the Somoza dictatorial regime. It achieved this objective in 1979 and established a new form of government in Nicaragua, ruling until 1990. Since that time the Sandinista National Liberation Front has become a political party in Nicaragua, and its candidate was elected president in 2006.

Ejército Zapatista de Liberación Nacional (EZLN). The Zapatistas are a militant group based in Chiapas, Mexico. Formed in the mid-1990s, this group advocates equality, control over resources, and better services for the indigenous population in Mexico. Although initially an armed group, the Zapatistas changed their strategy in the 1990s to reach out to the international community and nongovernmental organizations to pressure the Mexican government, rather than using weapons and guerrilla warfare.

Notably, we chose these groups because they illustrate the range of activities that women terrorists have engaged in over the history of modern terrorism. Women have been political vanguards for their movements, provided logistical support to terrorist groups, acted as recruiters by encouraging their brothers and sons to join, and fought side-by-side with men to achieve their objectives and win their cause. So it is worthwhile to explore all of these roles, rather than just focusing on one or two. Moreover, it is often said that history is told through the eyes of powerful men. The same could be said for the history of terrorist groups and terrorism in general. So it is perhaps worthwhile to pursue an alternative perspective—a feminine perspective—on why individuals join terrorist organizations and how they fight for their political causes.

DEFINING TERRORISM

Before we can explore why women join and the roles that women play once they become members of terrorist groups, it is perhaps useful to start with a basic understanding of the terrorist phenomenon itself. After all, individuals and militant organizations have been engaged in terrorism, as a form of political violence, for centuries. Terrorism scholars, such as David Rapoport and Bruce Hoffman, have traced religiously motivated terrorism to the Jewish Zealots' battle against the Roman Empire in AD 66–67. Yet most scholars agree that the 1968 hijacking of the Israeli El Al commercial airliner by Palestinians marked the advent of modern terrorism. Following this attack, author Walter Laqueur published *Terrorism* and observed that the term could be traced to a supplement of the *Dictionnaire* of the Académie Française, which was published in 1789, almost two centuries prior to the advent of "modern terrorism." The *Dictionnaire* supplement defined terrorism as *système, régime de la terreur*.[3] Thus, Laqueur argued that even in its earliest form, the term implied political upheaval, chaos, and violence.

Laqueur's study also provided a lengthy discussion of potential definitions of terrorism and the use of violence by nonstate actors in order to coerce a society into accepting certain political goals. Having discussed militants ranging from the Zealots in Palestine (66 AD) to the Thugs in India (thirteenth century) to the Russian Revolution and the Klu Klux Klan in the United States, he concluded that "all specific definitions of terrorism have their shortcomings simply because reality is always richer (or more complicated) than any generalization."[4]

Despite this conclusion, Laqueur put forth three common, although less specific, characteristics of terrorism—violent tactics, nonstate actors, and political objectives—which, in turn, have formed the basis for most subsequent terrorism studies.[5] Although Laqueur's research arguably provided the basis for the emergence of "terrorism studies," as distinct from studies of revolution and war, subsequent works on terrorism continued to wrestle with how to define their topic. Perhaps the best example is the work by J. Bowyer Bell on the PIRA. After a career of almost forty years of writing and studying armed conflict, Bell introduced his final book on the PIRA with this comment:

> No one can come to the contemporary armed struggle innocent. In fact everyone shapes reality: perception is all. In this the scholar and the analyst are no different from the lethal volunteer in an armed struggle; seeing is believing. And one sees as one believes. The rebel is driven by a vision only the faithful can see, and this largely determines his world. The rebel underground is moulded in a special way not readily amenable to the methods of social scientists or the analysis of the threatened. They, the pragmatists or the scientific scholars, examine the same phenomenon and yet see differently from the involved, from the rebel. They, historians and policy analysts and political scientists, often see not through a glass darkly but with great precision and from a special angle ... Here, then, at the start are the necessary definitions, valid here but perhaps not valid elsewhere, even in the underground.[6]

Bell's ironic and almost weary statement about "necessary definitions" underscores the state of terrorism studies between the late 1970s and the late 1980s. Throughout this period, most authors engaged in the philosophical discussions of what exactly constitutes terrorism, but a consensus could not be reached. In the end, some consensus was reached that terrorists want "a lot of people watching and a lot of people listening, but not a lot of people dead."[7] This consensus has come under criticism in the post-9/11 world. Al-Qa'ida, for example, clearly wanted to kill a substantial number of people in the 11 September 2001 attacks. Thus, some might argue, terrorism studies went astray in the 1980s.

The argument that terrorism studies went astray in the 1980s is believable in retrospect, of course, but not necessarily accurate. Was expert consensus wrong in the 1980s and the existing research just did not reveal it? Or, has terrorism changed dramatically since that time, and subsequent scholars have not adequately challenged their predecessors so as to reveal it? The most likely answer to these questions is "yes, both." In the past, scholars tended to begin their work with a chapter or section that defined terrorism. Yet these same scholars could not seem to arrive at an accepted definition. Perhaps this paradox was due to the international political context of the time and the Cold War, which set up ideological differences between freedom fighters and terrorists. However, a struggle clearly existed within the academic community to come to terms with the phenomenon of modern terrorism.

After the Iranian Revolution in 1979 and Hizballah's subsequent attack on the U.S. Marine and French paratrooper barracks in 1983, the U.S. government and Reagan administration, in particular, reportedly began to focus more on terrorism, shifting attention away from its criminal characteristics to more of a military threat.[8] Nevertheless, the academic community did not appear to respond as quickly. David Rapoport attempted to address the weakness in terrorism studies in his 1988 (edited) publication, *Inside Terrorist Organizations*. Rapoport opened his book with the statement, "In 1969 when I began to prepare a series of lectures for the Canadian Broadcasting Corporation entitled *Assassination and Terrorism*, I struggled to find appropriate materials but could only discover a handful of items. Seventeen years later, Amos Lakos published a bibliography on the same subjects which contained 5,622 items in English alone!"[9] Having outlined the growth of terrorism studies, Rapoport continued on to criticize academia for isolating its research to terrorists' motivations and evolving tactics:

> Indeed, interviews with captured terrorists by academics seem to focus on motivation; virtually no questions are asked about organizational details and issues. It is also clear that public materials like pamphlets and

especially terrorist memoirs—terrorists seem almost compelled to write memoirs—which contain much information on these matters have not drawn much attention.[10]

Rapoport featured two major arguments in *Inside Terrorist Organizations*. The first argument was that terrorist organizations' behavior is consistent with rational-actor theories. Terrorist organizations operate until opportunity costs are too high. If terrorists fail, therefore, it is because states have removed any possibility of the terrorist to be "rewarded" for violence. The second argument, embodied by Martha Crenshaw's chapter "Theories of Terrorism" and expanded on in her book *Terrorism in Context*, is that terrorist group behavioral patterns are best understood in the context of organizational continuity and survival. Failure, therefore, is not as much strategic as it is organizational—being a part of the terrorist group provides members with its own rewards distinct from the group's ability to ultimately achieve its stated political objective. In fact, the organization's leaders may be reluctant to see its purpose accomplished and the organization's utility ended. They are likely to see incremental gains sufficient to sustain group morale but not to end the members' dependence on the organization.[11]

Two years later, Walter Reich answered Rapoport's criticism with his own edited publication, *Origins of Terrorism: Psychologies, Ideologies, Theologies, States of Mind*. In this book, Reich, a psychologist, featured select articles by individuals outside the normal terrorism "expert" arena, such as Albert Bandura, a social psychologist who drew on studies of the Holocaust in his chapter "The Mechanisms of Moral Disengagement." Similarly, Martin Kramer's chapter "The Moral Logic of Hizballah" presented a unique look at Hizballah's leadership, focusing on how Hizballah viewed its campaign vis-à-vis Israel, but also within Lebanon. Finally, Ehud Sprinzak contributed a chapter on the development of the extreme left and the Weathermen in the United States. Thus, the literature moved away from a somewhat isolated and exclusive focus on terrorism studies, broadening the research focus and returning it to its origins in studies of revolutions and civil wars. Sprinzak's subsequent work on Gush Emunim and the Jewish Underground perhaps best illustrated this return.[12] In 1991, Sprinzak published an article in *Terrorism and Violence*, one of two journals dedicated to terrorism.[13] He wrote:

> Terrorism implies a crisis of legitimacy. What terrorists do—and other radicals do not—is to bring their rejection of the regime's legitimacy to the point of challenging it with unconventional violence. However, since terrorism never emerges overnight, this crisis of legitimacy unfolds through a prolonged process of delegitimation of the established society and the regime.[14]

In this article, Sprinzak continued on to argue against conventional wisdom in the academic community that terrorists are a fringe group, isolated from the beliefs and concerns of the wider population, but rather, he believed that terrorists emerge out of a wider radical political movement.[15]

Importantly, this shift did not occur in isolation, but was influenced by emerging studies on mass movements. At this point, it is worth noting that some social movement scholars have delved into terrorism studies and vice versa. One of the crossover scholars from the mid-1990s was the Italian sociologist Donatella della Porta. As part of her research, della Porta interviewed over 1,200 Red Brigade members and coded their activities from 1970 to 1983. She concluded that the RB gradually conducted more and more violent attacks not, as many argued at the time, to escalate the conflict, but rather as part of the RB's competition with other underground organizations for new recruits.[16] She also argued that social interactions, rather than individual characteristics, provide a more significant explanation as to why people join and remain a part of terrorist groups.[17]

Bruce Hoffman's 1998 book, *Inside Terrorism,* perhaps best represents the next significant collection of work on terrorism. Highly regarded both in academic and policy-making communities, Hoffman made three major contributions to the terrorism literature. First, he introduced his publication, not by defining terrorism (as his chapter title suggests), but by describing what terrorism is not. By adopting this approach, Hoffman could then emphasize the changing nature of terrorism over time. He concluded, "The terrorist campaign is like a shark in the water: it must keep moving forward—no matter how slowly or incrementally—or die."[18]

Second, Hoffman placed considerable emphasis on the rhetoric of terrorist organizations' leaders. For example, Hoffman cited ceremonial liturgy by the Phineas Priesthood (a white supremacist, antiabortionist group in the United States) as well as books written by Shoko Asahara, the leader of Aum Shinrikyo (the group responsible for the 1995 Tokyo subway nerve gas attack). Hoffman stressed the importance of understanding the terrorist phenomenon through the eyes of the terrorist leaders and their supporters. Finally, Hoffman explored the trend of terrorists with a religious ideology becoming more violent than their left-wing counterparts. He called into question the principle that terrorists "do not want a lot of people dead," especially religious terrorists, pointing out that international terrorism had progressively become more violent in the 1990s.

The last few years of the twentieth century might have marked the point at which the academic community began to truly engage in interdisciplinary and intradisciplinary debates on the topic of terrorism. This possibility is borne out by initial arguments on religious terrorism: some scholars supported Bruce Hoffman's contention that religious terrorists were more violent *because* of their ideological worldview, while others, such as John Esposito, argued that religion merely provided the rhetoric—as communism did during the Cold War—to disenfranchised groups.[19]

Mark Juergensmeyer's 2001 publication, *Terror in the Mind of God*, addressed this disagreement.[20] Juergensmeyer built his study of religious violence both on historical studies of terrorist organizations as well as on sociological theories of religion. His conclusions supported John Esposito's theory, except in certain circumstances. That is, Juergensmeyer argued that real-world violence takes on sacred meaning (versus terrorists conveniently adopting religious rhetoric) under three conditions:

1. The struggle is perceived as a defense of basic identity and dignity;
2. Losing the struggle would be unthinkable; and
3. The struggle is blocked and cannot be won in real time or in real terms.[21]

It is arguable that in a post-9/11 world, commentators, especially those in the Western world, have stopped viewing terrorism as part of a mass movement with certain goals and rational choices made to achieve these goals. Instead, in response to the horror of the attacks on the World Trade Center and Pentagon, books tend to emphasize the extreme and seemingly irrational. The challenge of studying and writing about terrorism in a post-9/11 world therefore sets the context for this book. In examining the roles that women have played in terrorists groups, we have attempted to go beyond the moral judgments of "terrorist" versus "freedom fighters." We find these moral arguments somewhat less interesting than the real day-to-day decisions that women have to make as they consider whether or not to join a terrorist group, as well as their actions once they have joined. Thus, we have returned to the basic definition of terrorism established by Walter Laqueur in the 1970s: terrorism is an act of violence committed by nonstate actors against civilian populations in order to achieve a political objective.

Examining women as terrorists, however, also necessitates an understanding of the wider political movements that these women are part of, including both the political movement of the terrorist groups as well as the feminist movement that so often influences their decision making. In this sense, our research into women terrorists does not indicate any differences between women and men or between religious women or secular women. The main differences arise not in the minds of women, but in the minds of the male leadership of terrorist groups— are they willing to put women on the front lines, or not? *Women as Terrorists* therefore addresses the most important questions in terrorism studies today as well as in the past: what motivates individuals to engage in terrorist activities? And how do terrorist groups make decisions? The difference between this book and those previously mentioned is that the answers come through the eyes of women terrorists.

UNDERSTANDING TERRORIST MOTIVATIONS

Why do people become terrorists? This question has been asked over and over again by multiple terrorism scholars over the past thirty years and the history of modern terrorism. Based on that research, a body of knowledge has begun to emerge on why and how individuals become involved with terrorist groups. Of course, experts might disagree as to the degree of significance for various factors that influence individuals to become terrorists, but certain factors have arisen repeatedly and, thus, tend to be viewed as more significant than others. As a result, experts have come to apply three different analytical frameworks to the question of why people become terrorists. That is, some experts emphasize structural causes or political, economic, or social grievances that prompt anger and motivate individuals.[22] It has also been demonstrated repeatedly that individuals join terrorist groups as part of social networks—friends persuade friends to become terrorists.[23] And, finally, it is clear that individuals do not just wake up one morning and decide to become terrorists, but rather they go through radicalization processes that move them from being upset to "picking up a gun" in pursuit of some political objective.[24] The following sections discuss these analytical frameworks in greater depth, applying them specifically to women.

Some people believe that a collection of grievances—political, economic, and social—prompt individuals to take violent action against the state. Hamas, for example, would like to see the creation of an independent Palestinian state. So it makes sense that individuals would join Hamas, at least in part, because they too share political grievances against the state of Israel. Of course, other Palestinian terrorist groups also fight for the creation of an independent Palestinian state. The Al-Aqsa Martyrs' Brigades, for example, as discussed above, represents a militant offshoot of the secularist-nationalist Palestinian group Fatah. In contrast to Fatah, Hamas advocates for an *Islamic* Palestinian state. It stands to reason, therefore, that Hamas supporters would be more sympathetic to the social grievances articulated by Hamas, and its proposed religious solutions, than al-Aqsa

Martyrs' Brigades. Other reasons might come into play for individuals as they choose to join Hamas; for example, Hamas might have provided them with food aid in the past, but grievances against the Israeli state also have an influence.

Other terrorist groups have articulated different grievances in justification of their violent campaigns. FARC, for example, emphasizes divisions between rural and urban, rich and poor, in Colombia, as part of its Marxist–Leninist agenda. Even al-Qa'ida articulates grievances against the Western world and Arab governments. For example, Osama bin Laden argued that the Western world had perpetuated or at least permitted massacres against Muslims around the world as his rationale for a declaration of jihad against the West in May 1996:

> It is no secret to you, my brothers, that the people of Islam have been afflicted with oppression, hostility, and injustice by the Judeo-Christian alliance and its supporters. This shows our enemies' belief that Muslims' blood is the cheapest and that their property and wealth is merely loot. Your blood has been spilt in Palestine and Iraq, and the horrific images of the massacre in Qana in Lebanon are still fresh in people's minds. The massacres that have taken place in Tajikistan, Burma, Kashmir, Assam, the Philippines, Patani, Ogaden, Somalia, Eritrea, Chechnya, and Bosnia-Herzegovina send shivers down our spines and stir up our passions. All this has happened before the eyes and ears of the world, but the blatant imperial arrogance of America, under the cover of the immoral United Nations, has prevented the dispossessed from arming themselves.[25]

Logically, these grievances affect women in the same way that they do men. That is, particularly with political grievances, one would expect women to be equally motivated to (e.g.) free themselves from an occupying force as would men. In her autobiography, *My People Shall Live*, one of the most infamous Palestinian terrorists, Leila Khaled, wrote of her struggle to receive approval from her parents to join in the fight against Israel in the 1960s:

> When we were kicked out of Palestine, they [leaders of the Arab Nationalist Movement] argued, Zionists did not distinguish between men and women. Women constituted over one half of the Palestinian people and they too were exiled. The Israelis trained their women to fight and granted them civil liberties. If we wished to defeat the Israelis we must outplay them in their own game.[26]

This somewhat egalitarian view of Palestinian grievances, however, did not exactly translate into equality for Palestinian women in society or even within the revolution. Women often have a more substantial array of grievances to rebel against than men. For women, therefore, the fight against oppression or to address these grievances within the state also can be a fight for greater quality within their own immediate community. Leila Khaled made a similar observation in her autobiography, stating, "I was terribly disturbed by their male chauvinism and self-righteousness.... How could we liberate Palestine and the Arab homeland, if we ourselves were not liberated? How could we advocate equality and keep over half—the female half—of the human race in bondage?"[27]

Nevertheless, the presence of grievances alone does not appear to be an adequate explanation for why people become terrorists. Wide arrays of grievances exist in a number of societies that have not seen the development of terrorism. Given this logic, terrorist groups should have a higher proportion of the female cadre than the male cadre, because women experience a higher proportion of oppression in general. That certainly is not the case, and so there must be other reasons why individuals and women in particular become terrorists.

Others believe that individuals join terrorist groups as part of a social network: friends persuade friends, brothers persuade sisters, and uncles persuade nephews to join terrorist organizations. Members of the "Virginia Jihad," for example, arrested for planning to travel to Afghanistan to fight against U.S. forces there in the wake of the September 2001 attacks, all attended the same mosque and socialized together, and many even trained together at paintball facilities.[28] Similarly, British Muslims responsible for the July 2005 attacks against subways in London allegedly came together through their membership in a sports club and allegedly went rafting together prior to this attack.

Some evidence suggests that women have been drawn into terrorist groups through their relationships with family, friends, and even lovers. The most notorious example is Anne Marie Murphy, who was stopped at Heathrow Airport in April 1986 because security guards found explosives in her carry-on bag. Apparently unbeknownst to Murphy, her fiancé, Nezar Hindawi, planted the bomb in her bag. This example, however, is more the exception than the rule. More typically, women appear to join terrorist groups because their friends and families are associated with those same groups.

Indeed, in her study of women members of the Basque terrorist group ETA, Carrie Hamilton observed that women became increasingly involved in this group in the mid-1960s. Although women mostly played a supporting role in ETA, by the early 1980s approximately 8 percent of ETA prisoners (imprisoned for political and militant activities) were women.[29] Hamilton interviewed thirty women members of ETA and found that many of them came to join the group under the influence of their fathers.[30] That is, daughters worshipped their father's role in resisting the state and thus followed in their footsteps. Similarly, in her book

Shoot the Women First, Eileen MacDonald interviewed two sisters associated with the political wing of the Basque terrorist group ETA. From these sisters' accounts, the eldest joined first, soon to be followed by her younger sister.[31] Thus, some evidence suggests that social networks and social influence apply to women recruits much in the same way that they apply to men.

It appears that women join terrorist groups for reasons very similar to those of men, both due to a desire to fight against grievances and due to the social influence of friends and family. Yet women often face recrimination by men within the revolutionary group as well as their immediate support communities for taking on such an aggressive role and risking their own lives. In this sense, women terrorists are forced to reconfirm their choice on a daily basis. Women's motivations, therefore, are perhaps best understood as a radicalization process, rather than a one-time choice to join or not join a terrorist organization.

Indeed, we understand radicalization processes to have three separate components. The first component, termed *availability*, incorporates those social, cultural, and other environmental contexts that make certain individuals vulnerable to clandestine movements. In his work on the psychology of terrorism, Clark McCauley notes that German research into the Baader-Meinhof Gang determined that, in comparative studies, those terrorists did not demonstrate higher rates of psychopathology than nonterrorists.[32] By using the term availability, therefore, we do not mean to suggest that individuals who become terrorists are psychopaths, without moral feeling. Rather, availability designates those circumstances surrounding individuals before they come into contact with the militant group itself. These circumstances might include discrimination and oppression, as indicated by the story told by Leila Khaled, as well as a fight for recognition as women within a wider political movement.

The second component of the radicalization process, *recruitment and indoctrination*, occurs after initial contact between individuals and the clandestine organization. So fathers might introduce daughters, friends might introduce friends, and sisters might introduce sisters. As mentioned above, the recruitment and indoctrination of women seems to parallel that of men as well. Donatella della Porta's study of the RB in Italy, for example, revealed that many members of the RB joined under the influence of peers and family.[33] Marc Sageman's more recent work on al-Qa'ida, titled *Understanding Terrorist Networks*, indicated that many members of al-Qa'ida have strong familial ties within the organization.[34] Importantly, this second component of the radicalization process does not necessarily have to include top-down recruitment by the clandestine organization itself. Sometimes individuals might seek out terrorist groups and volunteer, and in other instances individuals might be recruited for a specific role or mission.

Finally, we term the last component of the radicalization process *action*. At this stage, individuals have joined a clandestine organization and begun to take part in illegal activities to support the group. These activities might include financial or logistical support, but they also include a commitment to violence. Evidence suggests that many women terrorists have similar experiences to men at this stage as well. For example, North Korean Kim Hyon Hui was arrested for her role in a state-sponsored attack against Korean Air Flight 858 in 1987 that killed all 115 people on board. According to her autobiography, Kim was recruited by the government for undercover activities while at university and was subjected to indoctrination that included physical deprivation and emotional isolation for approximately seven years.[35] This indoctrination process laid the foundation for Kim's eventual willingness to conduct a terrorist attack, and while Kim's case was extreme, examples exist of terrorist recruits being subjected to indoctrination in training camps, including those found in Afghanistan, Sudan, and Sri Lanka. In other instances, recruits might be sent off to participate in a skirmish with state forces as a testing ground for their readiness and loyalty. For the most part, research suggests that women are tested in the same way as men. These types of experiences both reinforce and solidify an individual's commitment to the terrorist organization and its cause and, therefore, must be considered part of the reason why individuals become (and remain) terrorists.

In sum, studies of terrorists' motivations need to address a variety of influential factors to be complete, and these factors apply equally to men and to women. These studies ought to explore the political, economic, and social grievances articulated by terrorist groups and their followers. Additionally, the social networks ought to be examined to see if family members or friends played a role in influencing recruits' decisions to seek out and join terrorist groups. Finally, these studies ought to go beyond reasons and networks to examine the processes that individuals go through once they've made contact with a terrorist group that might influence their decision to remain. However, these factors only tell part of the story of women terrorists. We next turn to the issue of how terrorist organizations and their leadership have assigned different roles to their women members.

EXPLORING TERRORIST DECISION MAKING

If one crucial aspect of the concept of women as terrorists is an understanding of how women actually become terrorists, another is an understanding of how terrorist leaders use women recruits in pursuit of their objectives. Just as women's motivations fall within a wider context of motivations and causes, so too does terrorist decision making. In this sense, terrorist decision making can be viewed as a combination of *strategic thinking* and *opportunism.*

Some terrorist groups have evidenced a great deal of strategic thinking in their choice of targets and the tactics they use to hit those targets. For example, al-Qa'ida documents captured in Afghanistan in the wake of Operation Enduring Freedom suggest that al-Qa'ida leaders debated with their members on the efficacy of confronting U.S. forces in Somalia in the early 1990s. At that time, al-Qa'ida leadership determined that if it could confront American forces in Somalia successfully, the U.S. government would withdraw from the Muslim world entirely. And so, Osama bin Laden sent some of his followers to Somalia to confront the United States there. Operatives in Somalia subsequently sent a letter to al-Qa'ida leadership in Sudan in September 1993, complaining that the Somali fighters did not have a unified objective.[36] Al-Qa'ida leaders responded as follows, "When you entered Somalia, the Somali arena was barren and futile," the epistle's author wrote:

The situation changed, however, after the intervention by America and the Knights of the Cross. You most resembled a hunter aiming his rifle at the dead branch of a tree, with no leaves or birds on it. Suddenly, a bald eagle lands on the branch of the tree, directly in line with the rifle. Shouldn't the hunter pull the trigger to kill the eagle or at least bloody it?

The American bald eagle has landed within range of our rifles. You can kill it or leave it permanently disfigured. If you do that, you will have saved Sudan, Yemen, Bab al-Mandab, the Red Sea, the Arabian Gulf and the waters of the Nile. Could you want more magnificent objectives of war than those?[37]

Other examples exist of al-Qa'ida's strategic thinking, especially when it comes to personnel. Al-Qa'ida, or JI for al-Qa'ida, apparently recruited Malaysian biologist Yazid Sufaat specifically in the hopes that he would be able to forward their biological weapons program. Trials and captured documents also suggest that al-Qa'ida has sought to recruit members who can more easily get into the United States and Europe, because of their citizenship and passports.[38]

Other terrorist groups similarly have evidenced strategic thinking when it comes to the use and deployment of certain personnel. Hizballah, for example, has established sports camps in southern Lebanon and the Bekka Valley. Hizballah fought to remove Israeli forces from southern Lebanon in the 1980s and 1990s. After Israeli withdrawal in May 2000, Hizballah continued to expand its activities into Lebanese politics, but it did not give up its weapons. Supposedly, Hizballah uses its sports camps to determine the most athletic individuals and therefore the most desirable recruits.[39] It also attempted to work with Palestinian terrorist groups during the al-Aqsa Intifada to influence their choice of tactics and targets, sending some of its operational planners to the West Bank and Gaza Strip and urging local Palestinian terrorist groups to be more strategic than opportunistic.[40] The LTTE in Sri Lanka similarly implemented a filtering system to identify the best and most determined fighters that then would be selected to become Black Tiger suicide units.[41] Al-Qa'ida, Lebanese Hizballah, and the LTTE are all known by terrorism experts to be some of the most adaptive terrorist and insurgent groups operating today. So it seems clear that the strategic choice and utilization of key personnel is a characteristic of adaptive and dangerous militant groups.

In this context, the role women play in terrorist organizations could be the result of strategic decision making. Perhaps women can more easily penetrate security barriers or hide suicide-bombing vests. Indeed, in the case of Palestinian terrorist groups, women sometimes have been assigned as "handlers" to male suicide bombers. Palestinian terrorist leaders apparently believe that men are less likely to be thoroughly searched if they are accompanied by women, supposedly their wives or sisters.[42] The PIRA similarly used women to run bombs between operational cells in the belief that they were better able to avoid suspicion.[43]

Sometimes, however, terrorist groups behave more opportunistically than strategically, and moreover, their decisions are based on internal group dynamics rather than the best way to achieve strategic objectives. For example, the Jewish Underground was a terrorist organization that operated in the West Bank between 1980 and 1984. It began in response to the decision by Israeli Prime Minster Menachem Begin to sign the Camp David Accords. Members of the Jewish Underground—twenty-seven in all—believed that Israel should annex Judea and Samaria and believed that the reason for Menachem Begin's faulty decision, as well as the moral failures of Israeli society, could be laid at the feet of the Dome of the Rock. That is, they believed that the Dome of the Rock, built on top of the Temple Mount, needed to be destroyed:

> My friend argued that the existence of the abomination [Dome of the Rock] on the Temple Mount, our holiest place, was the root cause of all spiritual errors of our generation and the basis of Ishmael's [the Arabs'] hold on Eretz Israel.[44]

And yet, the Jewish Underground's terrorist activities were diverted from this objective. On 3 May 1980 Arabs attacked a group of Hebron Yeshiva students, killing six and wounding several more. Jewish Underground leaders subsequently met to discuss this incident and the overall increase in Arab violence against Jewish settlers. They decided to set aside their plans to attack the Dome of the Rock and instead engage in terrorist attacks against Palestinian Arabs, committing the following acts:

- June 1980: The Jewish Underground attempted to blow up the cars of five prominent Arab leaders. Two bombs went of successfully, crippling Mayor Bassam of Nablus and Mayor Karin Khalef of Ramallah. An Israeli demolition expert accidentally exploded a third bomb meant to injure the mayor of El Bireh and was seriously wounded.
- July 1983: The Jewish Underground attacked the Islamic College of Hebron, killing three students and wounding an additional thirty-three.
- April 1984: The Jewish Underground attempted to place bombs on five Arab buses in East Jerusalem. They were arrested at this time by the Israeli Secret Service.

These examples illustrate how terrorist leaders often choose their targets based on opportunity, rather than in an effort to pursue their overarching strategy. Sometimes, as was the case with the Jewish Underground, this opportunism can detract from the terrorist campaign, but in other circumstances it just adds to the fear caused in society by terrorist attacks.

In the same way, some terrorist groups reportedly are selective about the recruits that they accept into the organization, while others cannot afford to be as selective. Hamas leaders, apparently, prefer to use women as recruiters and logisticians, rather than as fighters or operatives. Because Hamas does not have a problem attracting new recruits, it has been able to divert women recruits into these roles. In contrast, evidence suggests that al-Aqsa Martyrs' Brigades has had more difficulty attracting more recruits, which might account for its willingness to accept women as suicide bombers. Similar arguments have been made to explain the presence of women suicide bombers in Iraq. So it is clear that both factors—strategic thinking and opportunism—can affect terrorist leaders' decisions on how and why they use women as part of their terrorist campaign.

CONCLUSION

It is clear that multiple factors can affect an individual's decision to join a terrorist group. These factors might include family ties and peer group relationships, as well as personal grievances and the structural characteristics of his or her immediate surroundings. In the same way,

multiple factors also influence the internal dynamics and decision making of terrorist groups. These factors might include the strategic objectives of a terrorist group or opportunities that present themselves to
terrorist leaders. The issue of women as terrorists, therefore, can be
understood at an individual level—why do women join terrorist
groups? But also at an organizational level—how and why do terrorist
groups deploy women? And, finally, at a community level—how do
women terrorists interact with their wider community? Although this
study by no means lays claim to be a definitive study on women as terrorists, it attempts to address all three levels of analysis. In this sense, it
provides insight into the immediate topic of women as terrorists and
the book also provides insight into the terrorist phenomenon in general.

2

Women as Logisticians

Women predominantly have played the role of logistician in terrorist groups. Indeed, for this study, we examined twenty-two different terrorist and insurgent groups that have incorporated women to some degree since 1968. Twenty-one of those terrorist and insurgent groups utilized women as logisticians. According to the Merriam-Webster Online Dictionary, logistics relate to the "procurement, maintenance, and transportation of military material, facilities, and personnel; the handling of the details of an operation."[1] For terrorist or insurgent groups, logisticians smuggle weapons and funds to terrorist fighters or perhaps act as couriers with messages between terrorist leaders and their operational cells. A number of explanations exist for the fact that women more often than not play the role of logistician. For one, it seems that terrorist leaders often believe that women are less suspicious and less vulnerable to inspection by security authorities. By having women smuggle weapons, therefore, terrorist leaders think they increase the likelihood that the weapons will be delivered safely. So it is not unheard of for terrorist leaders to have women hide and deliver explosives in baby carriages—the epitome of innocent womanhood.

Similarly, it appears that some terrorist leaders believe logisticians are exposed to less danger than operatives, and thus it is a more suitable role for women. This logic is not unique to terrorist leaders, of course. Many national leaders have expressed some reluctance to incorporate women into their military structures, for instance, or if women are part of the military, they often are given noncombatant roles. Nevertheless, this logic or belief seems somewhat misplaced, for the lines between combatant and noncombatant for a terrorist organization often get blurred. For example, counterterrorism officials frequently target the logistical and support networks of terrorist groups. These networks are targeted because they are essential for the sustainment of a terrorist campaign. This counterterrorism approach, however, also means that women logisticians risk arrest and retaliation, just like terrorist fighters or operatives.

Finally, some terrorist groups only accept full-time operatives. These full-time operatives live clandestincly and so are not able to interact regularly with family and friends. Therefore, individuals with family obligations, who still want to be part of a terrorist group in these circumstances, often are given part-time supportive roles in logistics. This full-time versus part-time division of labor applies equally to men and women, yet women are more likely to have family responsibilities, such as child care, and so often are relegated to support tasks. It is logical, in this context, that because more women take on "part-time" roles in terrorist groups, more women would be placed into logistical roles than tasked with guerrilla, suicide, or other terrorist attacks.

Some women, of course, have fought against this historical pattern and become fighters and operatives in terrorist groups. Leila Khaled, a female operative for the Popular Front for the Liberation of Palestine (PFLP), for example, told about her efforts to become a fighter for Fatah, Yasser Arafat's militant wing of the Palestine Liberation Organization (PLO) in the late 1960s. Even from a young age Leila Khaled, who resided in Palestinian refugee camps inside Lebanon, was involved in activist groups. Yet she aspired to be a resistance fighter. Despite her desire to become a fighter for Fatah, according to Leila Khaled's autobiography, *My People Shall Live*, Fatah cast women primarily as fundraisers.

> Fatah was something new in my experience. Our [women's] sole function was fund-raising. We were not a part of the policy-making processes, but merely spectators or ticket agents in the temple of Fatah ... I began to press for answers ... I wanted to know what women could do beyond fund-raising?[2]

In her frustration, Leila Khaled left Fatah and joined the PFLP, which promised that she could eventually become a fighter once she had proven herself trustworthy and capable. Twenty other women joined Leila Khaled at the PFLP military training camp in Lebanon, according to her account. Yet not all of them became fighters for this terrorist group. She explained this attrition as follows:

> If a woman decided to commit herself to this phase of the revolution [military training], it meant the final break with her past and relegating her private life and desires to a secondary position. If she was unable to accept these terms, then she could make a partial commitment to becoming a supporter or a friend of the resistance rather than train to become a professional revolutionary.[3]

Leila Khaled's autobiography is particularly interesting in this regard because she expressed a great deal of scorn for those women who did not choose to forsake their past and become a fully committed professional revolutionary. As such, the autobiography likely reflects a generally held belief among both men and women supporters of terrorist groups that individuals who prefer to take on less risk in pursuit of the terrorist group's objectives are perhaps less worthy or committed. Indeed, other first-hand accounts told by women terrorists also reveal struggles against this mindset as they tried to contribute to terrorist groups' objectives in their own ways.[4]

Despite Leila Khaled's insistence that from her perspective only fighters truly contributed to the Palestinian resistance during the 1970s and 1980s, our research into women as logisticians suggests that this role was not necessarily any safer than that of fighter and that it was not less crucial to the terrorist group as a whole, nor were women logisticians any less devoted to the terrorists' cause. Women logisticians risked arrest or even death to smuggle weapons and protect fighters. These women also worked diligently to keep society functioning, particularly difficult in an environment where many husbands and fathers were in prison or operating clandestinely. Thus, it is fair to say that the backbones of resistance movements are often the logisticians, and in many circumstances women logisticians. These women clearly have contributed to the overall success of terrorist campaigns and yet received little acknowledgement from terrorist leaders or even from society—men, women, or children—for their sacrifices. Interestingly, as counterterrorism officials, this finding gives us pause to a certain extent, because it suggests that efforts to win over the "hearts and minds" of a population should be focused at least to a certain degree on the women in society, rather than exclusively on their husbands, brothers, and sons.

For the most part, women logisticians have adopted three basic tasks in support of a terrorist group's objectives. The first basic task is that of courier. The most common responsibility for couriers has been to transport money and weapons between different members of the terrorist group. Couriers also smuggle messages between terrorist leaders as well as between terrorist leaders and their supporters. Perhaps less common, but no less significant, couriers sometimes build bombs and help operatives smuggle firearms away from the target after an attack takes place. By separating the firearms from the shooter, women couriers help mitigate the possibility of arrest and incarceration. In this context, couriers not only provide the terrorist operatives with supplies, but also help minimize the risk that the operatives face from security authorities after an attack.

The second task is that of protector. "Protector" is not necessarily an official position within a terrorist group, but we decided to capture this role because it is relevant to women in communities that support terrorist movements. Protectors provide safe houses for terrorist operatives as they are attempting to escape capture by security authorities. They also visit terrorist detainees in prison, sometimes smuggling in messages and sometimes simply helping to keep up the terrorists' spirits because they are removed from their families and comrades. In this last role, protectors often risk arrest or retaliation for smuggling messages into and out of prisons. Similarly, women's organizations that are suspected of providing support to terrorist groups also are targeted for arrest or reprisal by security officials. So being a protector is not an easy task.

The third and final task often adopted by women logisticians is that of "decoy." Sometimes terrorist leaders have used women to distract and confuse security authorities in the midst of an attack. For example, women have lured security officials into the arms of waiting assassins. Women also have escorted suicide bombers to their targets, deflecting attention away from the bombers because security officials view them as part of a "couple" and so are less of a threat. This responsibility is perhaps the least common for women logisticians, but it is one of the most disturbing. Like the baby carriages filled with explosives, women decoys take advantage of their seeming innocence, but the attacks are much more personal—for example, the assassination of a policeman interested in a pretty girl. In each of these tasks, women logisticians have attempted to help their respective terrorist movement achieve its political, military, and even economic goals. Sometimes it is arguable that their responsibilities were more difficult and burdensome than the fighters.

COURIERS

When people think of women as logisticians in terrorist groups, they often picture women couriers, and it is true that women often take on the role of courier for terrorist groups. For example, in the late 1950s, women helped in the resistance against French colonial rule in Algeria. Veiled and unveiled, Algerian women were able to more easily move among the French soldiers, carrying revolvers, grenades, and false identity cards for the underground movement.[5] Indeed, the well-regarded 1966 movie *Battle of Algiers* featured women couriers as part of its story about the insurgency against French forces in Algeria. In this movie, these Algerian women easily smuggled bombs through French security checkpoints, while their male counterparts were searched, captured, and arrested. This movie, therefore, provides a powerful representation of the logic behind terrorist leaders' use of women as logisticians. In the specific case of the Algerian separatists the movie also was a reflection of reality.

During the 1987 Palestinian Intifada, women similarly smuggled leaflets to shopkeepers and other neighborhood leaders to help coordinate mass demonstrations against the Israeli security authorities.[6] Sometimes hidden in babies' diapers, these leaflets also let people know the dates for workers' strikes and when it would be better to stay off the streets.[7] In fact, because of their prominent role as couriers in the Intifada, women's rights became a topic of debate in the Palestinian territories at that time.[8] Several leaflets issued by Palestinian activists associated with Fatah and the PLO addressed the important role that Palestinian women were playing in the uprising. Some of these leaflets mentioned women prisoners,[9] whereas others urged women to participate in sit-ins and protests.[10] In March 1988, similarly, one leaflet praised women's efforts in the uprising and stated, "O masses of the valiant PLO, great glory and esteem to the woman for her devotion and generosity to her people...."[11] Indeed, the role of women as weapons smugglers and leaflet couriers is evident throughout the history of terrorism.

Beyond smuggling leaflets and weapons, women have also been used by terrorist groups as fundraisers and money smugglers. In her book on Palestinian women, *Army of Roses*, Barbara Victor observed that Palestinian women have smuggled money across the border between Jordan and Israel for terrorist groups.[12] According to Israel security authorities, approximately twenty-five Palestinian women were arrested over a period of six months during the al-Aqsa Intifada, each smuggling more than US$10,000.[13] The smuggling of funds into the Palestinian territories was particularly important for terrorists during the al-Aqsa Intifada, as Israeli counterterrorism forces instituted closures throughout the area in an effort to reduce the number of suicide bombings and other attacks originating from the West Bank and Gaza Strip. So it makes sense that Palestinian terrorist groups would attempt to utilize women to smuggle funds, anticipating that they would be less susceptible to close scrutiny and searches.

Similarly, in her article "Cross-Regional Trends in Female Terrorism," Karla Cunningham observed that Kurdish terrorist groups based in Turkey have used women refugees in Kurdish Diaspora communities as fundraisers.[14] The Partiya Karkerên Kurdistan (PKK), or Kurdish Workers' Party, fights for the establishment of an independent Kurdish state in territory that overlaps Turkey and Iraq. One of the PKK's founding members, Kesire Yildirim, was a woman, and the PKK reportedly had more than 1,100 female fighters at one point. Yet the PKK also used women as logisticians to support its fight for independence. For example, PKK women fundraisers in the Kurdish Diaspora include

Hanan Ahmed Osman, who was granted refugee status by Canada in 1984, and Zehra Saygili, who helped raise and smuggle money for the PKK in the late 1990s as part of the Kurdish Cultural Association in Montreal.[15]

Hizballah also has used women to raise funds in support of its terrorist campaign against Israel. Hizballah is a Shi'ite organization based in Lebanon. For almost two decades, between 1983 and 2000, Hizballah fought against an Israeli military presence in southern Lebanon. Israel withdrew from southern Lebanon in May 2000, and the fighting between Hizballah and Israeli security forces subsided for several years until the summer of 2006. In 2006, Hizballah members kidnapped several Israeli soldiers, and Israel retaliated by invading southern Lebanon. This invasion and the subsequent violence threw Lebanon into a downward spiral of instability for the next two years. Prior to and during this struggle in 2006, Lebanese women raised funds in support of Hizballah through the Islamic Resistance Support Association. To do this, women sewed garments to be sold and arranged community dinners. They also created a "sponsor a fighter" program that allowed women to provide directly to specific Hizballah fighters.[16] Indeed, women's role of fundraiser and money smuggler is evident across all different types of terrorist groups.

Women often have risked arrest or worse as part of their smuggling operations. The Provisional Irish Republican Army (PIRA), in particular, utilized women extensively as couriers, and many of them ended up in prison. Cumann na mBhan was formed by members of the original IRA, the precursor to the PIRA, in 1913 as a women's auxiliary branch. Women in the Cumann na mBhan acted as nurses, couriers, and often intelligence gatherers for the fighters during the mid-twentieth century. Beginning in the late 1960s and early 1970s, however, women began to take a more active role in the PIRA, smuggling bombs in baby carriages and hiding weapons in their homes. As the role of women increased, so did their exposure and the potential risk for arrest.

For example, in her book *Only the Rivers Run Free*, Eileen Fairweather tells the story of "Rose," who joined Sinn Fein, the political front for the PIRA, with her husband. After his death at the hands of British security forces, Rose apparently took on a more active role in the clandestine militant activities of the PIRA. Rose was arrested in 1974 and charged with possession of a weapon and then rearrested in 1977 when security forces discovered five incendiary devices in her home.[17] In fact, by 1981, thirty-six women associated with the PIRA were in Armagh Women's Prison on a variety of terrorism-related charges.[18]

Beyond the movement of money, messages, or weapons, women also have helped to build improvised explosive devices and, in the case of

Palestinian women, suicide belts. For example, Eileen Fairweather also recounts interviews with female PIRA volunteers (versus Cumaan na mBhan) in the 1980s:

> Another [female] volunteer was surprisingly frank about her involvement, telling us, "I work with explosives." We were even more surprised when the person who accompanied her during the interview interjected to say, "She's just being modest when she says that. She's one of our top explosives experts, one of the best we have in the movement." Without any hint of false modesty, she continued as if this had not in fact been mentioned, "You see, we have women who work in all spheres—the carrying of weapons, planting bombs, making them, setting up operations, carrying out the jobs, bringing the weapons, and getting them away after the job.... When I first joined I was used for scouting and courier work. Then when I began to build up a rapport with my male comrades my work expanded."[19]

This statement provides particular insight into the role of women within the PIRA and perhaps terrorist groups in general. It explicitly demonstrates the range of tasks given to women, ranging from smugglers to bomb makers to operatives to planners, but it also suggests that women were allowed to demonstrate their prowess, beginning their jobs as PIRA volunteers with courier work and working their way up with more and more responsibilities if they chose.

The experience of women in the PIRA mirrors stories contained in Leila Khaled's autobiography of her experiences with the PFLP, as well as other accounts told by female terrorists in the Revolutionary Armed Forces of Colombia (FARC). Indeed, many of the women that we discuss as suicide operatives and guerrilla fighters in Chapters 4 and 5 originally began their careers as couriers. That is, women might have joined their respective terrorist or insurgent groups as couriers, but as they proved themselves willing and able to be responsible for terrorist attacks themselves, they were essentially "promoted" within the organizational structure. This promotion led women to take on the role of, somewhat ironically, suicide operative or guerrilla fighter.

Nevertheless, couriers have not always been promoted to fighters; some instead have become commanders of logistical networks. "Sonia" represents perhaps one of the more unique examples of a female logistician who advanced to a leadership position within a militant organization. At the time of her arrest, Sonia was thirty-seven years old and had been a member of the FARC since she was a teenager. FARC is a Marxist–Leninist group that operates in Colombia and since the 1990s has become heavily involved in the drug economy. Sonia came from a poor peasant family and joined the FARC after two years of middle school, according to an interview with Sonia posted on a Spanish Web site.[20] Also known by other names, such as Anayibe Rojas Valderrama and Omaira Rojas Cabrera, Sonia was captured by the Colombia security forces in February 2004 and extradited to the United States in 2005. Sonia was a commander in FARC's 14th Front and oversaw roughly half of FARC's drug trafficking activities, earning the FARC tens of millions of dollars on an annual basis.[21] In this sense, Sonia represents an alternative promotion structure within a militant group that has engaged in terrorist activities. Rather than being promoted from courier to bomb maker to fighter, as was the case in the PIRA, Sonia was given more and more responsibility within FARC's drug-running and logistical networks.

Interestingly, al-Qa'ida also has used women as couriers in its history of terrorist attacks against the United States and other Western targets. In June 2002, for example, security authorities in Morocco arrested six individuals and accused them of plotting to attack American and British ships in the Straits of Gibraltar.[22] The al-Qa'ida plan apparently was to crash small boats filled with explosives into the hulls of these ships to sink or immobilize them, as occurred in the October 2000 al-Qa'ida attack against the USS *Cole*. The three businessmen arrested for this plot were originally from Saudi Arabia. They had traveled to Morocco and married local women to help establish their residency.[23] Although the men ultimately would have conducted this attack, the investigation led Moroccan authorities to claim that their wives collected and transferred funds, purchased the small boats, and generally acted as couriers for this al-Qa'ida cell.[24]

Other examples of women acting as couriers also exist from al-Qa'ida. Since 2001, U.S. security authorities have claimed that Iran has held some al-Qa'ida deputies in that country under house arrest. Although Iran has released some of these operatives to Saudi Arabia, others remain, including individuals referred to as Said al-Adel and Mahfouz Ould Walid. These two men have been accused by U.S. and Arab security authorities for helping to plan the 1998 al-Qa'ida attacks against the U.S. embassies in Kenya and Tanzania, among other operations.[25] Questions arise, of course, as to the relationship between these individuals, other al-Qa'ida operatives in the Middle East, and the senior leadership of al-Qa'ida in the Afghanistan–Pakistan border. Yet, according to U.S. security officials, women have been used as couriers to pass information between al-Qa'ida operatives in Iran and other countries, because they can more easily cross borders.[26]

The use of women as couriers by al-Qa'ida is particularly intriguing, because Ayman al-Zawahiri, the second-in-command for al-Qa'ida, has claimed that women should not play these roles in the fight against the

West. Indeed, in December 2007, Ayman al-Zawahiri offered to answer questions posted by supporters on several Web sites known to be sympathetic to al-Qa'ida. Ayman al-Zawahiri received thousands of questions relating to al-Qa'ida activities in Iraq, Afghanistan, and North Africa; al-Qa'ida's relationship with Hamas (Harakat al-Muqawama al-Islamiyya); the justification of suicide bombings; and even what terrorist groups should be considered part of al-Qa'ida. Women also posted questions to Ayman al-Zawahiri, asking about their appropriate roles in the al-Qa'ida campaign. Al-Zawahiri responded that women should not join the ranks of al-Qa'ida operatives and that their best role in this campaign was to endure the hardships presented by husbands who fight for al-Qa'ida and to raise their children appropriately.[27] Al-Zawahiri's answer clearly did not align with reality on the ground. It may have reflected his ideal, rather than a general al-Qa'ida policy. At the very least, it suggests that even cultural and religious conservatism can be overlooked by midlevel leaders and operatives, especially if they need women to provide logistical and other forms of support to pursue a terrorist campaign.

In sum, two patterns in terrorist and insurgent groups' use of women couriers appear evident. The first pattern includes women recruited as general members and then allowed to work within the terrorist organization structure to find tasks and responsibilities best suited to them. The PIRA in Northern Ireland, PFLP in the Palestinian territories, and FARC in Colombia exemplify this pattern. Women in these organizations were initially recruited to be part of the support network, but they were allowed to expand their roles and responsibility by proving themselves over time.

The second pattern includes women recruited for specific tasks and courier missions. In this later instance, women retained the same basic role as they initially were given or perhaps were only used a few times by the terrorist organization. Examples of this type emerged in our analysis of Hizballah in Lebanon, the PKK in Turkey, and al-Qa'ida. While it might be tempting to conclude from this analysis that secular terrorist groups provide women with greater opportunities to expand their responsibilities, this conclusion is too preliminary because it does not account for the other roles that women might play in these groups, such as recruiters, operatives, and vanguards, which we address in other chapters. It is interesting, however, to observe that sometimes terrorist groups seek out women to act as couriers, while at other times women choose to become couriers as a general means to contribute to the fight.

The next section continues our exploration of women as logisticians by focusing on one of the least understood roles, that of protector.

PROTECTORS

Although women couriers clearly have contributed to the ability of terrorist groups to plan and execute their campaigns over the years,
women also have taken on the role of protectors within their respective
societies. As protectors, women often have used their femininity to confound security authorities or place them in awkward positions where
they would have to go against culturally acceptable behavior. In these
circumstances, the male police or military officials often back off and
cede a certain degree of power to the women logistician. This role can
prove essential to the overall survival of any given terrorist operative,
but it can also help the terrorist group itself remain diligent in the face
of counterterrorism pressure.

For example, a number of stories have been told about the courage and
ingenuity of Palestinian women during the 1987 Intifada. One story in particular illustrates how women have taken on the role of protector whether
or not they have official membership in a terrorist group. In this story, a
young man in the Gaza Strip was caught throwing stones at Israeli soldiers. The soldiers chased him down and began dragging the young Palestinian man toward their jeep. A young woman with a baby in her arms
reportedly rushed up, yelling, not at the soldiers, but at the young man,
"So there you are! I told you not to come into town today! I told you there
would be trouble! And what do you expect me to do while you are
arrested? How will I eat? How will I feed our baby? I am tired of your
irresponsibility to your family! I will not do it alone! Here, you take the
baby and try to feed her!"[28] The young woman then dumped her child
into the arms of the Palestinian man and ran away. The Israeli soldiers
were reportedly so bewildered they left the man, got in their jeep, and
drove away. The young woman then reappeared to retrieve her child—she
and the Palestinian man were complete strangers.[29]

Truth or fiction, this story illustrates how women have used their inherent power within society to protect potential terrorist operatives in
the Palestinian territories. Palestinian women also worked tirelessly to
keep the momentum going for the Palestinian resistance movement during the first Intifada. For example, Palestinian women's committees
quickly emerged to help provide logistical support to the protests during the 1987 Intifada. These activities included arranging demonstrations, organizing emergency aid and relief to the refugee camps, hiring
lawyers for detainees, and visiting the families of martyrs. In her article
"Palestinian Women in the Intifada," Naila Daniel observed that by
March 1988 approximately 115 demonstrations per week had been
organized by Palestinian women.[30] These demonstrations, for the most
part nonviolent, formed the core of the Intifada. Security authorities

were taken aback by the high level of participation in these demonstrations as well as their longevity. Yet Palestinian terrorist groups continued to garner support for their marches and strikes. And women played an important role in the success and continuity of these demonstrations. They were more easily organized by women because they could move around more freely than Palestinian men.

In response to the 1987 Intifada demonstrations, Israeli security forces instituted curfews and closures throughout the Palestinian territories. The purpose of these closures was twofold: first, to limit Palestinians' ability to move from village to village and therefore gather for demonstrations; and second, to apply economic pressure on the Palestinian community to reduce their support for the demonstrations. Palestinian women responded to the curfews and closures by stockpiling food. Women's committees then organized a smuggling network to get food and other items into those areas hit hardest by the curfews and closures. Women also visited families in their neighborhoods, known to be passive in the Palestinian resistance, to encourage their participation in the strikes and demonstrations.[31]

In this way, the efforts of women "protectors" in the Palestinian territories helped to minimize the effectiveness of Israeli counterterrorism measures. They used their status in society to protect young male activists, provide aid to communities being punished for harboring terrorists, and cajole passive supporters to become activists. Indeed, women's contribution to the momentum of the 1987 Intifada was significant enough that in August 1988, the Israeli government banned Palestinian women's organizations and neighborhood committees.[32]

Similar efforts were made by Irish Republican women in Northern Ireland and the conflict with England. For example, in 1981, PIRA detainees went on a hunger strike to protest the conditions at Long Kesh and Crumlin Road Jail as well as in an effort to reclaim their status as political prisoners rather than basic criminals. This hunger strike often is viewed as one of the key events that led to the eventual 1998 Good Friday Accords, paving the way for peace in Northern Ireland. In the lead-up to these hunger strikes, approximately 550 PIRA detainees in Long Kesh and Crumlin Road Jail had gone "on the blanket" or had refused to wear prison clothes in protest of their change in status from political prisoners to criminals.[33] To support these detainees, mothers and wives in the Republican movement created the Relatives Action Committee, which organized demonstrations and helped families who had fathers and husbands in prison.[34]

Women prisoners also played a role in the "on the blanket" protest and eventual hunger strikes. At that time, thirty-six PIRA women detainees lived in Armagh Women's Prison. Three of these women decided that they too would go on a hunger strike in December 1980.

These women included Mairead Farrell (the leader of the PIRA female detainees at the time), Mary Doyle, and Margaret Nugent. Four years later, Farrell described the situation and her decision to go on strike as follows:

> There'd been a lot of pressure on us not to go on the hunger-strike from the Republican movement outside, and we'd given in to it for a bit. But the situation was so bad in here, and when the men went on hunger-strike we felt we'd no other option but to join them after having held back for so long.[35]

Ten men eventually would die from hunger in these strikes, including Bobby Sands, whose funeral was attended by approximately 100,000 individuals. Bobby Sands's sister would subsequently use her notoriety gained from his death to form the Real Irish Republican Army in protest of the Good Friday Accords (see Chapter 6). Although no women died in the strikes, their willingness and contribution drew media attention, which added to the pressure on the central government in London. The strikes also mobilized popular support for Sinn Fein and the PIRA in Northern Ireland, with strikers becoming celebrities and eventually candidates for election.

Finally, women also have played the role of protector for al-Qa'ida and affiliated terrorist groups, particularly in Afghanistan, Indonesia, and Iraq. These women have acted as protectors in slightly different ways than those presented above, in Northern Ireland and the Palestinian territories. Al-Qa'ida leaders have asked their fighters and operatives to marry women from local families and tribes in order to secure their support and protection for al-Qa'ida members. In this way, al-Qa'ida wives protect their husbands and other fighters indirectly through the relationship itself, rather than directly through their actions.

For example, it is well known that in 2008 al-Qa'ida reconstituted a network of fighters and supporters in the border area between Pakistan and Afghanistan. Part of this network was built upon familial relationships between al-Qa'ida fighters and local tribes. As al-Qa'ida solidified these relationships through marriage, tribes became increasingly loyal and protective over al-Qa'ida fighters. Indeed, al-Qa'ida even assigned one of its members, Sufi Abdul Aziz Baba, to take care of the widows and children of al-Qa'ida fighters in Afghanistan. Not only were these women protected by Sufi Abdul Aziz Baba, but they were trained to fight in case they were captured by Afghani tribal leaders in partner with the U.S. military and its allies.[36]

In a similar pattern, Jemaah Islamiyya (JI) pursued an agenda parallel to al-Qa'ida in Southeast Asia between the late 1990s and 2008: it wanted to see a Caliphate in the region ruled by Islamic principles and laws. This terrorist group was responsible for two separate attacks against Western tourists in Bali (October 2002 and 2005), as well as attacks on the Marriott Hotel and Australian Embassy in Jakarta, Indonesia. And, like al-Qa'ida, JI reached out to other Muslim insurgent groups and local cells throughout the region in an effort to coordinate their activities, including the Moro Islamic Liberation Front and the Abu Sayyaf Group in the southern Philippines, as well as operational cells in Malaysia, Singapore, and Australia. According to studies on JI conducted by the International Crisis Group in Indonesia, its leaders solidified loyalty from its members as well as surrounding communities through marriage.[37]

Of course, sometimes this approach of obtaining protection through marriage to local women has backfired against al-Qa'ida and affiliated terrorist groups. Al-Qa'ida in Iraq (AQI), for example, attempted to marry its foreign fighters into local Sunni tribes in al-Anbar province in 2005 and 2006. Apparently, al-Qa'ida in Iraq (AQI) arranged their marriages in an effort to solidify relationships with local tribes, following the model established in Afghanistan. Over time, however, AQI's approach turned too aggressive and abusive. That is, AQI attempted to impose its strict religious beliefs and teachings on tribal families in al-Anbar and even coerce marriages. Local Sunni leaders resented the fact that younger, teenaged girls were forced to marry al-Qa'ida foreign fighters. This resentment eventually contributed to al-Anbar's pacification and the Sons of al-Anbar militias that worked with U.S. security forces against al-Qa'ida in that province.[38]

In sum, when examining women as logisticians, or indeed even women as terrorists, authors tend to focus on couriers and fighters, but leave out the role of protectors. Yet this role is clearly both challenging and dangerous to women in societies that support terrorist groups. Moreover, in many ways, women as protectors help to minimize the dangers posed by security authorities to male operatives and help to bolster and sustain community support for the terrorist groups. This support, in turn, allows the terrorist group to continue to recruit new members and provides materials and safe havens for the operatives themselves. It is therefore a noteworthy role, both to students of the terrorism phenomenon and to counterterrorism officials.

The next section further examines the roles that women play as logisticians, focusing specifically on women as decoys.

DECOYS

The final task that women often take on as logistician is that of decoy. It is somehow easy to accept women couriers whose primary responsibilities are to smuggle weapons or protect detainees from harm. Women decoys, however, present a troubling image. These women take advantage of their seemingly innocent status in society to distract security officials from their duties or even lure them to harm. Indeed, women have confounded security officials repeatedly in their roles as decoys, and so it is logical that terrorist leaders would continue to deploy them in this way.

For example, Ahlam Tamimi was a twenty-year-old student at Birzeit University when she became a handler or controller for Palestinian suicide bombers. According to Barbara Victor, in her book *Army of Roses,* Ahlam Tamimi (whom Victor refers to as Zina) was living with her family in Jordan when she became pregnant outside of marriage.[39] Her child was taken away from her by her father, and it was determined that it would be raised as her brother's son. Soon thereafter, Tamimi was sent by her family to Birzeit University in the Palestinian territories, both to further her education but also so that she could redeem herself by providing support to Fatah, the militant branch of former President Arafat's PLO. While at Birzeit University, however, Tamimi met an active member of Hamas and persuaded him to nominate her for membership.[40] Hamas rarely accepted women, but Tamimi must have provided her abilities and loyalty, because she was chosen to be a handler for a suicide attack on 9 August 2001.

On 9 August 2001, Tamimi left Ramallah with twenty-three-year-old Izzadine al-Masri for downtown Jerusalem. She was chosen to accompany al-Masri because a couple traveling together was likely to be less suspicious than a young man traveling by himself.[41] Because Tamimi had a Jordanian passport, she could more easily travel through the checkpoints in public transportation along the way and, thus, carried the explosives, while al-Masri had to walk on foot around several checkpoints. The attack killed fifteen people and wounded an additional 130. Tamimi eventually was arrested for her role in the attack and imprisoned, along with approximately 100 other Palestinian women, for her membership in a terrorist organization. After her arrest, she told Israeli security authorities that she had conducted surveillance of the target prior to the actual suicide bombing, taken pictures with her camera, and had consciously spoken English to al-Masri so that they could appear as tourists.[42]

Other examples of women decoys exist outside the Palestinian territories. According to Eileen MacDonald, for example, Cuman na mBahn women sometimes purposefully attracted British soldiers with sexual advances only to lure them to a secluded spot where they could be killed by IRA gunmen.[43] The Baader-Meinhof Gang in Germany also used women as decoys. Also known as the Red Army Faction, the Baader-Meinhof Gang was a terrorist organization that emerged from the communist youth movements in the 1960s. Women played a significant role in this group as leaders, operators, and also decoys. For example, in September 1977, the Baader-Meinhof Gang kidnapped Hanns-Martin Schleyer, president of the Employer's Association and of the Federation of German Industry. Schleyer was riding in his chauffeured car to work one morning when a woman with a baby carriage stepped in front of his vehicle. The chauffeur stopped the car, and while the car was stopped, Baader-Meinhof members grabbed Schleyer, holding him for forty-three days before they killed him.[44]

Similarly, Andrea Klump was a key operative for the Baader-Meinhof Gang in the 1980s, but she also acted as a decoy on multiple occasions. In 1985, for example, she reportedly lured a U.S. soldier to his death in order to steal his identity card.[45] The Baader-Meinhof Gang needed this identity card so that they could more easily access and attack a U.S. military base in Frankfurt. So this attack reflected not only creative planning in the use of women as decoys, but also forethought and strategic thinking versus opportunism. In fact, in August 1985, the Baader-Meinhof Gang detonated a car bomb at this base, killing two individuals and wounding another sixteen.

More recently, the Groupe Islamique Arme (GIA) in Algeria also used a woman as a decoy for its planned, and failed, Millennium plot against the United States.[46] The GIA is an insurgent group that operates in Algeria, but has articulated a local Islamic agenda similar to al-Qa'ida's global agenda. Lucia Garofalo, age thirty-five and a resident of Montreal, was used to smuggle GIA members across the border between Canada and the United States. She was arrested at the Vermont border attempting to bring an Algerian man named Bouabide Chamchi, with a false French passport, into the United States. Interestingly, the vehicle that Garofalo was driving at the time of her arrest was registered to another Algerian, Brahim Mahdi, suspected of ties to the GIA.[47] According to BBC News, authorities suspected that she became associated with the GIA through her husband, an Algerian man deported from Canada for using a false passport and suspected of having ties to the Algerian terrorist group.[48]

Finally, it is worth mentioning a somewhat different role that women have played as decoys for al-Qa'ida. In April 2008, security authorities in Mauritania arrested Maarouf Ould Hadib, a member of al-Qa'ida. Hadib apparently orchestrated an attack against French tourists in Mauritania in December 2007. The tourists had stopped for a picnic outside the capital when al-Qa'ida terrorists shot them. Mauritania's authorities subsequently began a search for foreign terrorists responsible for this attack and eventually captured Maarouf Ould Hadib. According to a government spokesman, Maarouf Ould Hadib was disguised as a woman when he was arrested.[49]

In sum, a variety of different terrorist groups—ranging from the Islamists to leftists to nationalists—have used women as decoys in order to further the success of their operations. Some rare cases also have male terrorists dressing as women in order to avoid capture. Women, in this sense, clearly are less suspicious and so better able to slip past security officials or even lure them into danger. Some examples, such as the Baader-Meinhof Gang, suggest that these women still take on the roles of fighters as appropriate. In other examples, however, women appear specifically assigned only to the role of decoy. Perhaps as interesting, family pressure (especially in the cases of Tamimi and Garofalo) appears to have influenced these women as they decided to adopt the responsibility of "decoy" for the terrorist organization. That is not to say that women are more likely to be motivated by these personal relationships than men, as our study did not really compare the two possibilities, but rather that at least women appear to be willing to assume a certain degree of risk to please their husbands and families.

CONCLUSION

This chapter explored how and why terrorist organizations have used women as logisticians to further their political, economic, and social objectives. To do this, we discovered that women have been used as logisticians in a significant and diverse number of terrorist groups, including al-Qa'ida in Afghanistan and Iraq; al-Qa'ida in the Islamic Maghreb; JI in Indonesia; Fatah, Hamas, and PFLP in the Palestinian territories; Hizballah in Lebanon; GIA in Algeria; PKK in Turkey; FARC in Colombia; the PIRA in Northern Ireland; and the Baader-Meinhof Gang in Germany. In fact, of the twenty-two different terrorist and insurgent groups examined in this book, twenty-one utilized women as logisticians. These various terrorist groups also have spanned a number of decades, from the left-wing groups of the 1960s and 1970s to Islamic militant groups operating in the twenty-first century. Indeed, women have made significant contributions to their respective terrorist groups as logisticians.

Yet, it is interesting to note that even though the role of logistician is most frequently attributed to women, it is rarely discussed in the existing literature on women terrorists. Instead, most studies focus on women suicide bombers or women guerrilla fighters. Perhaps the topic of women as suicide bombers is more controversial, and so it is a more exciting topic. Alternatively, this absence arguably can be understood, at least in part, as contributing to the overall lack of understanding for the role that women play in terrorist organizations and their contribution to the terrorist movement in general. Of course, women sometimes are promoted within the terrorist organization, moving from courier or decoy to terrorist operative or sometimes being promoted within the ranks of logisticians themselves. One could assume that these promotions—as within any organization—are the result of merit, reliability, and interpersonal relationships, but that is unclear. Some women appear to have chosen to remain fairly low-level logisticians, whereas others ambitiously have sought to become major players in their terrorist organization. Additionally, it is clear that family, friends, and even tribal connections also contribute to the role of women logisticians in terrorist groups, sometimes removing the choice from the hands of the women themselves in the first place.

Indeed, this chapter also underscores how very little we know about the internal workings of terrorist groups and the opportunities afforded to men or women within their structures. If we understood these internal dynamics better, perhaps we would gain greater insight into why some individuals join and remain terrorists for years if not decades.

3

Women as Recruiters

Beyond logistician, women also have played the role of recruiter in terrorist and insurgent groups. Recruiters are individuals used or designated by terrorist leaders to attract new logisticians, financiers, suicide bombers, or guerrilla fighters into their organization. Recruiters also often serve as essential linkages between a terrorist or insurgent groups and popular support communities. Of the twenty-two different terrorist and insurgent groups in this study, seven utilized women as recruiters. So this role is much less significant for women than logistician, which manifested in twenty-one of the twenty-two terrorist and insurgent groups in this book. Partly, this lack could be explained by the observation that the membership of terrorist and insurgent groups is comprised primarily of men and, thus, it is logical for men to recruit other men. Nonetheless, women have taken on the role of recruiter, often by their own initiative, and so it is a useful point of comparison: why do women serve as logisticians more than as recruiters?

In some ways, the position of "recruiter" in a terrorist group is similar to that of "logistician" in the sense that these individuals are not in the direct line of fire from counter-terrorism security forces. In fact, recruiters often operate well below the radar and, thus, are unlikely to be exposed to risk, even to the degree of risk assumed by logisticians in a terrorist group. Additionally, it is difficult for counter-terrorism and security officials to justify efforts to capture or kill recruiters, since they often do not engage in violent activities themselves. Yet recruiters make an important, or arguably essential, contribution to the overall success of a terrorist group.

The logic behind terrorist leaders' use of women as recruiters, however, is less straightforward than women as logisticians. One might argue that recruiters assume less of a risk than logisticians, suicide operatives, or guerrilla fighters, and so terrorist leaders might think this a safer task. Indeed, some of our examples in this chapter suggest that women were used as recruiters at first because terrorist leaders did not know quite what to do with the female volunteers. Beyond the issue of risk, however, we also found in our research that women recruiters tend to make potential male recruits feel somewhat guilty for remaining on the sidelines: if women are willing to assume risk, it is wrong culturally in many societies for men to remain safe. Finally, women sometimes teach their sons and daughters that terrorism is worthwhile and justi-fied, suggesting an informal role of "recruitment" even if terrorist lead-ers do not consciously recognize or acknowledge it.

In general, two basic patterns of recruitment for terrorist and insur-gent groups exist. First, sometimes family members or friends encour-age potential new recruits to join a terrorist group. These family members might or might not be associated directly with the terrorist group, but they still facilitate the recruitment of new members. For example, one of the most notorious female suicide bombers in Iraq, Muriel Degauque, apparently joined al-Qa'ida in Iraq (AQI) with her husband. Degauque was from Belgium and converted to Islam after her first marriage to a Turkish immigrant. That marriage ended in divorce, but Deguaque subsequently married an Algerian immigrant and moved to Morocco with him, where the couple became connected to and joined AQI.[1] This pattern of wives being recruited by husbands, brothers being recruited by fathers, or sisters being recruited by brothers, has not been unusual for European recruits into al-Qa'ida. Indeed, in his 2006 study of 242 European al-Qa'ida fighters, Edwin Bakker found that 20 percent were related to the terrorist cell through kinship.[2]

Second, although the terrorist recruitment process often is facilitated by a family member, sometimes recruiters seek out specific individuals or skills that they need for an attack or even to fill a capability gap within the terrorist group as a whole. For example, Khalid al-Masri apparently acted as recruiter for al-Qa'ida's Hamburg Cell, many of whom ultimately were responsible for the 11 September 2001 attacks inside the United States. U.S. government officials in the spring of 2008 similarly identified Badran Turki Hishan al-Mazidih, otherwise known as Abu Ghadiyah, as a key facilitator of foreign fighters into Iraq for al-Qa'ida.[3] Most of these foreign fighters in Iraq were designated as sui-cide bombers and recruited specifically for martyrdom missions. Addi-tionally, Wadih el-Hage was an al-Qa'ida fighter who was captured and eventually convicted on terrorism charges for his part in the 1998 U.S. embassy bombings in Kenya and Tanzania. In his trial, Federal Bureau of Investigation agents testified that Wadih el-Hage was recruited into al-Qa'ida because he had a U.S. passport.[4] Al-Qa'ida leaders apparently believed that someone with a U.S. passport would be able to move more freely in the West. These examples illustrate how recruiters often target individuals for specific roles or because they evidence certain characteristics. Indeed, effective recruiters are essential to success of a terrorist group, because they allow terrorist leaders to increase both the quantity and quality of their fighters.

Of course, the majority of terrorists are recruited by men, as illustrated by the examples above, most likely because men continue to dominate the operational, leadership, and decision-making roles in terrorist groups.[5] Nevertheless, historical examples exist of women who have engaged directly in the recruitment of new male logisticians, financiers, suicide bombers, and guerrilla fighters for terrorist groups. Perhaps even more interesting, women sometimes facilitate the recruitment and membership of other women in their respective terrorist groups. This trend—women recruiting women—is less evident in the terrorist groups associated with al-Qa'ida. For example, a spokesperson for the U.S. military in Baghdad said in March 2008 that no evidence existed to suggest that women in Iraq were recruiting other women to become fighters or even suicide bombers.[6] Yet, examples of female recruiters exist in a number of other terrorist and insurgent groups, including the Sendero Luminoso, or the Shining Path, in Peru; the Revolutionary Armed Forces of Colombia (FARC); and the al-Aqsa Martyrs' Brigades in the West Bank and Gaza Strip, as well as the Provisional Irish Republican Army (PIRA) in Northern Ireland.

Like the role of logistician, information on female recruiters in terrorist groups, and specifically woman-to-woman recruitment efforts, is minimal at best, yet it appears that the role of women as recruiters can be important. Thus, we determined that it is worthy of a chapter in this book. To do this, the chapter examines three key ways that women enable recruitment into terrorist groups: facilitators, propagandists, and historical conscience. First, identified as "facilitators," women sometimes play a direct person-to-person role in the identification and recruitment of new members into a terrorist organization. These women may recruit guerrilla fighters, but also logisticians, financiers, or even new members slated for suicide missions, and that recruitment occurs through relationships built directly between the woman and potential new members.

Second, women recruiters also play a less direct role in the recruitment of individuals as they take on the role of "propagandists" in terrorist groups. Propagandists run Web sites or public events that cajole and persuade their male counterparts to join the fight against terrorist adversaries. Because no direct person-to-person relationship is formed by women in this role as propagandist, it is somewhat different from facilitator. Yet women as propagandists can be particularly effective because guilt appears to play a role in their recruitment efforts. Of course, this role dovetails somewhat with the fundraising discussed in Chapter 2, but we distinguish propaganda generated for fundraising (as discussed in the last chapter) from propaganda used for garnering more recruits discussed in this chapter.

Finally, we also discuss the role that women recruiters play as the "historical conscience" of their societies that, to a certain extent, nurtures and encourages violence. Although somewhat uncomfortable to discuss, it is worthwhile to note that women often tell stories of past grievances and wrongs to their children, and as such, pass along feelings of enmity that may translate into terrorism. This role has become particularly evident in places like Northern Ireland and the Palestinian territories, where violence has lasted for generations. So we thought it a role worth exploring further in Chapter 3.

FACILITATORS

Historically, women facilitators have recruited new members—men and women—for terrorist and insurgent groups in both rural and urban areas. Sometimes facilitators play a specific, designated role as recruiters. Yet, other times, this recruitment takes place through relationships built with brothers, sisters, husbands, or even with friends. Both of these methods—directed and selected recruitment—are important to the overall survival of a terrorist group. Moreover, women have taken on both methods of recruitment in their effort to be part of a functioning and successful terrorist group.

For example, the Shining Path, an insurgent group that operated in Peru during the 1960s, 1970s, 1980s, and 1990s, was founded by Abimael Guzmán in Ayacucho, a rural district in southeastern Peru.[7] Articulating a Marxist ideology, the Shining Path expanded its reach throughout rural Peru until its violence threatened the capital city, Lima, in the early 1990s. At its inception, Guzmán and the Shining Path relied heavily on women for recruitment activities. Guzmán himself was a professor at the University of Huamanga, and he built on his relationship with students to spread Marxist teachings. A number of his initial followers were women from the education department at the University of Huamanga. For these women, recruiting was a natural fit.[8]

Similarly, the FARC utilized women as recruiters to sustain its fight against Colombia's central government and security forces. Like the Shining Path, the FARC is a Marxist–Leninist group with roots in the country's rural districts and, in fact, controls territory in southwestern Colombia. It also became heavily involved in drug trafficking in the

1990s. FARC traditionally has used a combination of enticement and coercion to gain new members, particularly guerrilla fighters. While men have been heavily involved in these recruitment activities for the FARC, so, too, have women facilitators.

In September 2003, for example, the Human Rights Watch issued a report titled "You'll Learn Not to Cry: Child Combatants in Colombia." This report included a story about a FARC recruiter named "Angela." Angela was a member of the FARC for four years, and her primary roles were that of nurse and facilitator during that time period. In her role as facilitator, Angela recruited men, women, girls, and boys into FARC. She apparently felt guilty about her role as a recruiter, especially the coercion of young girls and boys into the FARC, stating the following:

> Once in 1999, we forced some kids to join. We told them we were with the guerrillas, and they said they didn't want to join, that they wanted to keep studying.
>   We said you're already with us; you can't leave. We were armed and we told them to come with us. There were ten or so of them, about sixteen to seventeen years old. They were terrified. But we needed people, so we brought them to camp in our truck. I felt really guilty.[9]

This example suggests that facilitators have used not only positive relationships to persuade new members to join their respective terrorist groups, but they are also not above coercion. This pattern of coercion plus persuasion applies equally to male and female facilitators. Importantly, during the period described above by Angela, the FARC was under significant pressure from Colombian security forces (aided through U.S. counter-narcotics funding) as well as armed paramilitary organizations. Thus, it is likely that FARC moved toward coercive recruitment measures as its need for volunteers began to exceed its supply.

Up to this point, all of our examples have focused on women facilitators as they recruited male guerrilla fighters for their respective insurgent or terrorist group, but women also have been recruited by other women to sacrifice for their cause. For example, Wafa al-Bis was a female Palestinian suicide bomber who was captured by Israeli security forces in June 2005, at the Erez border crossing between Israel and the Gaza Strip. As a resident of Jabaliya refugee camp, Wafa al-Bis's ultimate target was the Beer Sheva hospital across the border in Israel proper. Reportedly, Wafa al-Bis attempted to detonate her suicide vest once she was stopped by security officials at the checkpoint, but the device was faulty.[10] She claimed to be a member of the al-Aqsa Martyrs' Brigades, an offshoot of former President Yasser Arafat's Fatah organization. According to an interview, Wafa al-Bis was recruited by another woman and friend. Apparently, Wafa al-Bis's recruiter was not an official member of the al-Aqsa Martyrs' Brigades, but she was helping her brother, who worked for al-Aqsa Martyrs' as a facilitator for male suicide bombers.[11]

Outside the West Bank and Gaza Strip, a popular urban myth in Chechnya suggests that an older woman named Black Fatima, who wears black furs and has a hook nose, recruits and trains young women for suicide bombings. Chechen militants have fought against the presence of Russian security forces in their territory since the 1940s, but the violence recently reignited in the mid-1990s. As part of their militant activities, Black Widows, or female Chechen operatives, were used as suicide bombers. In this context, Black Fatima has been described and mentioned by families of female Chechen suicide bombers associated with the Dubrovka Theater in October 2002, as well as Russian security authorities. According to these authorities, Black Fatima also recruited Zarema Muzhikhoyeva to conduct a suicide attack against a Moscow restaurant in July 2003.[12] Notably, many experts have suggested that the Russian government fabricated Black Fatima as a way to explain why Chechen women are being drawn in increasing numbers to commit suicide bombings, rather than admit that it may be due to a host of societal factors, such as poverty and loss of relatives due to Russian "disappearance."[13] Nevertheless, the character of Black Fatima remains a powerful representative of how some societies perceive the importance of women facilitators to terrorist groups.

Finally, beyond Black Fatima, it seems clear that Chechen insurgents have managed to gather new female members not as much through top-down recruitment as through kinship ties. For example, according to Anne Speckhard, all of the women she analyzed for her study on female suicide bombers in Chechnya self-recruited early on in the process. That is, these women chose to become terrorists mostly on their own and found their way into the militant group through familial connections.[14] This pattern also was evident in Euskadi Ta Askatasuna (ETA), sometimes referred to as the Basque Fatherland and Freedom terrorist organization. This terrorist group was formed in the late 1950s as both a separatist movement in the Basque-controlled portion of Spain as well as a Marxist–Leninist group. In 2004, Spanish scholar Fernando Reinares released a study of 600 ETA members active in the terrorist group in the 1970s and 1980s. Men comprised 90 percent of Reinares' sample, or approximately 540 individuals. Nonetheless, in examining this data, Reinares concluded that a majority of the women ETA operatives (a total of sixty individuals in his dataset) had joined ETA through boyfriends or husbands.[15]

In sum, although relatively infrequent, some examples exist of women as facilitators in terrorist groups. These women engage with individuals who might be willing and able to fight for their respective terrorist and insurgent groups. Sometimes the women facilitators build on existing positive relationships with these possible recruits and persuade them to become a terrorist. These relationships more often than not are rooted in kinship ties. Indeed, the importance of kinship ties is prevalent not only in rural societies, such as Chechnya, but also in urban communities, such as those supporting ETA in Spain.

In other instances, however, women facilitators demonstrated a willingness to coerce their colleagues—male and female—into joining with a terrorist or insurgent group. We found stories of coercive measures for both the FARC in Colombia and the Sendero Luminoso in Peru, during the course of our analysis. Sometimes these coercive measures are used against young girls and boys, which seem to contradict the basic concept of women as nurturers. After all, it is likely that new recruits will die at the hands of security forces eventually, or at the very least spend significant time in jail, and yet, women facilitators have been willing to persuade and coerce young people in their communities to pick up a gun or even put on a suicide vest in pursuit of their cause.

Thus far, this chapter has focused on women facilitators, who build relationships with new recruits in order to improve the quality and quantity of fighters in their terrorist groups. The next section focuses on a less direct recruitment method utilized by women recruiters: propaganda.

PROPAGANDISTS

If facilitators engage with potential new recruits through either constructive or coercive relationships, then propagandists throw ideas out into the public in the hopes that they might inspire individuals to "pick up a gun," even though the propagandists might never meet these new recruits in person. Historically, propagandists have filled important roles in terrorist organizations, providing fodder for new recruits as well as mobilizing a general sympathy in support populations. For example, Abdullah Azzam released a series of pamphlets in the mid-1980s cajoling Arabs to help support the Afghanistan fight against Soviet invades. These pamphlets were distributed widely throughout the Muslim world under the name of *al-Jihad* and eventually formed the ideological as well as rational basis for al-Qa'ida.

Similarly, Abel Aziz Rantisi was considered one of Hamas's (Harakat al-Muqawama al-Islamiyya) top leaders beginning in the 1980s until he was assassinated by Israeli security forces in 2004. Rantisi was widely believed to be responsible for writing Hamas's leaflets that were distributed as propaganda during the 1987 Intifada against Israeli forces in the West Bank and Gaza Strip. These leaflets mobilized and directed supporters in their nonviolent demonstrations and strikes against Israel, but they also laid the foundation for Hamas's growth and expansion throughout the 1990s until their electoral victory in January 2006. Thus, propagandists can play an important albeit indirect role as recruiters for a terrorist organization.

In a few instances, women have taken on the role of propagandist for their respective terrorist or insurgent groups. For example, the Liberation Tigers of Tamil Eelam (LTTE) in Sri Lanka have used women as propagandists since the early 1980s. According to accounts posted on its Web site, the LTTE formed its women's wing, Vituthalai Pulikal Munani (Women's Front of the Liberation Tigers) in August 1983. Also know as Suthanthirap Paravaikal or Birds of Freedom, the LTTE Women's Front was responsible initially for propaganda and other support activities, although it eventually emerged as a funnel for female guerrilla fighters and suicide operatives. As propagandists, the LTTE Women's Front issued leaflets and materials on atrocities suffered by Tamils at the hands of the Sri Lankan government. This material served primarily a recruitment function. For instance, in their article on the Birds of Freedom published in November 2007, Kim Jordan and Miram Denov quoted an LTTE female cadre on the topic of recruitment propaganda as follows:

> The way the LTTE recruit people is very different from the way a traditional military would recruit.... They will have propaganda materials about how bad the government army is, how the occupation is making our land worse, how we are suffering.... [T]hey [encourage] the people to come together, on a voluntary basis. So typically, your son or daughter will be exposed to this material, and then someday you will see they are not there, they just disappear [to the LTTE].[16]

This quotation underscores how propaganda can help attract new members to a terrorist or insurgent group: it generates interest and reinforces animosity or prejudice. Nevertheless, it is worth noting that the LTTE did not rely solely on propaganda for its recruitment activities. Individual recruits instead were put through a fairly rigorous test of loyalty and indoctrination before they were officially brought into the organization. Allegations also have been made in the past that coercion plays a key role in LTTE recruitment. Having said that, it is clear from this example that the propaganda provided by the Women's Front of the LTTE contributed to the recruitment of new fighters for that insurgent group.

Al-Qa'ida also has benefited from women who have acted as propagandists for this terrorist group. Unlike the LTTE in Sri Lanka, women propagandists for al-Qa'ida do not appear to have been directed by al-Qa'ida senior leadership to take on this role. Rather, the role has been adopted on the initiative of al-Qa'ida female supporters themselves. For example, Malika Aroud was a Moroccan–Belgian woman who ran a Web site sympathetic to al-Qa'ida (http://minbar-sos.com). Aroud apparently experienced a stereotypical "Western" youth in Belgium, drinking and clubbing, until she came into contact with a Muslim women's group that was coincidentally occupying office space in her home in Switzerland. As a result of these interactions, Aroud reportedly returned to her Moroccan–Muslim roots and belief system. Interestingly, Aroud's husband, Abdessater Dahmane, was responsible for killing Northern Alliance leader Ahmad Shah Massod two days before the 11 September 2001 attacks, supposedly at the behest of al-Qa'ida. According to most experts, al-Qa'ida arranged to have Ahmad Shah Massod assassinated in an effort to secure Taliban support in the face of a potential U.S. invasion following the September 2001 attacks.

Malika Aroud traveled with Abdessater Dahmane to Afghanistan prior to September 2001 and lived with him in al-Qa'ida camps in that country. Although she did not engage in militant activities herself, as the wife of Massod's assassin, Malika Aroud garnered quite a bit of notoriety in the wider community of al-Qa'ida sympathizers. In a 2006 interview with CNN, Aroud described her feelings towards al-Qa'ida as follows, "Most Muslims love Osama. It was he who helped the oppressed. It was he who stood up against the biggest enemy in the world, the United States. We love him for that."[17] Malika Aroud subsequently married another al-Qa'ida fighter and wrote a book called *Soldiers of Light*. Through this book and her aforementioned Web site, Aroud has attempted to motivate other men and women to support al-Qa'ida in its fight against the United States and its allies in the West.[18]

Indeed, according to Karla Cunningham, "overall, women have become important agents for recruiting other members, especially women through the Internet."[19] The Internet has become an incredibly important tool for recruiting in the last decade, for both men and women. Women have formed their own chat groups, disseminate propaganda on behalf of their organizations, and solicit membership through the Web.[20] Cunningham says, "Women's use of, and influence over, technology has the potential to affect female standing within groups and their overall operational roles."[21]

Although not much is known about the level of women's involvement in technology-assisted recruitment other than the select few who run Internet magazines or chat rooms, there is some evidence that women, particularly those who are active in the al-Qa'ida movement, are enabling the resistance by participating in organizations or activities that serve as critical outreach for al-Qa'ida and other like-minded groups. Examples include fund-raising organizations, women's groups, distributing Korans in prison, participation in Islamic camps for young girls, and Muslim Student Associations (MSA) on university campuses.[22] Indeed, a number of women in Saudi Arabia also have formed something of a propagandist group for al-Qa'ida. These women call themselves Al-Qa'ida's Arabian Peninsula Women's Information Bureau and apparently have decided to raise support for al-Qa'ida among women in other parts of the Muslim world, as well as being an advocate for women to join al-Qa'ida as suicide operatives or guerrilla fighters. To promote these efforts, in August 2004, the Arabian Peninsula Women's Information Bureau started an online magazine called *Al-Khansaa*. This magazine was named after Islamic poetess Al-Khansaa bint Omar, who converted to Islam during the time of the Prophet Mohammed. Al-Khansaa also is known as the "mother of the shaheeds" (martyrs) for sacrificing four of her sons in battle. With its pretty pink and peach hues, al-Qa'ida's Arabian Peninsula Women's Information Bureau apparently designed this magazine to reach out and enlist women to become members of al-Qa'ida.

Al-Khansaa's first issue, for example, included articles on how to physically prepare for jihad as well as how to groom the next generation of children for al-Qa'ida's fight against the United States and its allies. Indeed, the inaugural issue proclaimed "We will stand ... with our weapons in our hands and our children in our arms."[23] Although *Al-Khansaa* articles have encouraged women not to shy away from al-Qa'ida's battlefield operations, it is important to note that the magazine's content also supports women's more traditional role in al-Qa'ida, emphasizing the crucial role that women play in society as the mothers of the next generation. The following statement was taken from an *Al-Khansaa* article:

> A woman in the family is a mother, wife, sister, and daughter. In society she is an educator, propagator, and preacher of Islam.... [J]ust as she defends her family from any possible aggression, she defends society from destructive thoughts and from ideological and moral deterioration....[24]

Significantly, this quotation parallels the opinion presented by Ayman al-Zawahiri, al-Qa'ida's deputy commander, in January 2008, on the role of women in al-Qa'ida. As discussed in Chapter 2, Ayman al-Zawahiri responded to questions about the appropriate role of women in al-Qa'ida at that time by arguing that al-Qa'ida did not utilize women fighters, but instead saw their role as surviving hardships and encouraging a new generation of al-Qa'ida fighters in their children. Indeed, women supporters of al-Qa'ida appear to have adopted this more standoff-ish role, despite their inquiries to al-Qa'ida's Web site in 2007 and 2008.

Nonetheless, one woman has risen to prominence in the wider al-Qa'ida movement, despite al-Zawahiri's denunciation and reluctance to claim that women play such a role. Most people refer to this woman as "Umm Usama" (the mother of Usama, a reference to Bin Laden). Although Umm Usama allies herself with al-Qa'ida, not much is known about her identity beyond the fact that she told London-based newspaper *Al-Sharq al-Awsat* in March 2003, "We are building a women's structure that will carry out operations that will make the U.S. forget its own name."[25] Umm Usama subsequently claimed that this "women's structure" was an all-female suicide unit. These statements are particularly interesting because they have spurred a series of discussions online by both male and female al-Qa'ida supporters. Significantly, a few men have written words of support online echoing that women have a right to participate in jihad, but the majority of men who participate in these online forums do not believe that women have a place in militant groups and that they should continue to support men by raising their children to become fighters.[26]

In sum, terrorist leaders draw new members into their groups through multiple channels. More often than not, new recruits are identified through direct person-to-person contact with a facilitator: male or female. Sometimes, however, these relationships are initiated or even reinforced through propaganda. Propaganda makes potential recruits curious about a particular terrorist organization, or it motivates these new recruits to "get off the fence" so to speak and seek out friends or family members who might be associated with a terrorist group. Some of the most well-known terrorist propagandists, such as Abdullah Azzam or Abdel Aziz Rantisi, have been men. Yet women also have been assigned or adopted the role of propagandist on their own initiative, including Umm Usama and Malika Aroud. In this sense, women have taken on an indirect role as recruiter.

HISTORICAL CONSCIENCE

Up to this point we have discussed women as facilitators, who form relationships with potential recruits to persuade or coerce them to join a terrorist group. We also have discussed women as propagandists, who use various forms of media to advocate for the use of violence in a particular country or against a particular adversary. Women as propagandists, in this sense, take on a less direct role in the recruitment of new terrorist members. Beyond these two tasks, women also have served as the historical conscience of their communities, and, as such, lay the foundation for young people to believe in a particular terrorist group's worldview and even become terrorists themselves. Even less direct than propagandists, this particular task is worth exploring because it contributes to a general feeling of sympathy and support for terrorism in local communities.

Indeed, women often serve as the historians and storytellers who pass along to future generations not only what has happened in their own families, but also what has occurred in their communities. As such, these women act as the historical conscience of their societies and in many ways serve as natural recruiters for terrorist and insurgent groups. Women as historical conscience do not directly facilitate the recruitment of new members into terrorist groups, nor do they function as propagandists within a terrorist or insurgent group. Instead, through their stories, women as historical conscience either knowingly or unknowingly lay the foundation for potential recruits to accept and perhaps even desire membership in a violent group.

This pattern apparently has arisen most often in societies where conflict has endured for generations. Many of the women in these societies have suffered personal abuse and deprivation. In this context, these mothers, wives, and sisters also harbored feelings of anger and revenge, passing these feelings and historical memory to their children. By passing along these feelings and memories, moreover, these women prepared generation after generation of young people to continue the "fight" for their particular ethnic or religious group. Because in many societies women are often perceived as honorable and principled, their support for a cause often brings moral weight. While not typically considered an official role by terrorist leaders, women acting as historical consciences can entrench enmity in a community and make resolution of the violent conflict very difficult.

For example, studies suggest that women in Northern Ireland have passed along cultural stereotypes that serve to entrench in their children hostile and suspicious attitudes between Republicans and Loyalists. In her work on the peace process in Northern Ireland, Valerie Morgan wrote about past and ongoing efforts to solidify the terms of the negotiated 1998 Good Friday Accords that set forth a plan for peace between the Republican and Loyalists. Morgan concluded:

> [Women in Northern Ireland] are often very powerful within the family as transmitters of culture. Here their wish to protect their families and particularly their children from violence frequently impels them towards peacemaking but this desire often co-exists with a commitment to preserve and transmit their own culture which may lead them consciously or unconsciously to pass on stereotyped and potentially divisive attitudes.[27]

Morgan's observations suggest that, even during times of relative peace, women in societies that have experienced significant conflict may directly or indirectly prepare their children to continue to fight by passing along cultural concepts of identity, which also include "us–them" mindsets. In perpetuating these distinctions and mindsets, moreover, these women likely believe they are protecting their homes, families, and way of life.[28] So it is difficult to persuade them to behave in a different manner.

Another example of women as the historical conscience of a society exists in the Palestinian territories. Palestinian mothers, wives, and sisters sometimes teach and reinforce the perception in the West Bank and Gaza Strip that it is acceptable and even desired to fight for the creation of a Palestinian state. In doing so, Palestinian women directly or indirectly encourage Palestinian youths to engage in terrorism against Israeli civilians. In fact, this role of women as the historical conscious of Palestinian children and potentially future terrorists is even mentioned in Hamas's charter:

> The Muslim woman has a role in the battle for the liberation which is no less than the role of the man for she is the factory of men. Her role in directing generations and training them is a big role. The enemies have realized her role: they think that if they can direct her and raise her the way they want, far from Islam, then they have won the battle....[29]
>
> The women in the house of the *Mujahid* (and the striving family), be she a mother or a sister, has the most important role in taking care of the home and raising children of ethical character and understanding that comes from Islam, and of training her children to perform religious obligations to prepare them for the *Jihadic* role that awaits them.[30]

These statements by terrorist leaders in the Palestinian territories are reinforced by the behavior of Palestinian mothers, sisters, and wives. For example, when a Palestinian man or woman martyrs himself or herself, women often ululate[31] and pass out candy and coffee to celebrate the martyr's entrance into heaven, solidifying for the children at home watching that killing oneself in the name of Islam and in pursuit of a Palestinian state is an honorable and desirable act. Partly as a result of this acceptance and reinforcement by Palestinian mothers, sisters, and wives, a culture of martyrdom has emerged in recent years that reinforces for men who martyr themselves, the rewards are great: honor through defending the Palestinian people, fulfillment of duty to God, black-eyed virgins in the afterlife, and security for the family he leaves behind.[32]

Notably, most people tend to refer to "cultures of martyrdom" specifically for Muslims communities, such as the Palestinian territories, Egypt, Saudi Arabia, or even Lebanon. While terrorist groups clearly have utilized suicide bombers in these societies, other cultures of martyrdom have emerged and been reinforced in non-Muslim societies as well. Perhaps the most prevalent society that has glorified suicide terrorism is the Tamil community, controlled by the LTTE, in Sri Lanka. A nationalist-separatist group, the LTTE has used suicide operatives more regularly than any other militant group and over a longer period of time. As in the Palestinian territories, moreover, martyrs are celebrated as heroes in Tamil communities. For example, posters glorifying these martyrs reportedly could be found throughout Tamil territory in Sri Lanka during the 1990s and in the twenty-first century, and videos of their exploits could be viewed and purchased online. The LTTE reportedly today still monitors its guerrilla fighters and picks the most loyal to become suicide operatives, which generally has been considered an honor among the families and operatives. Indeed, even among those LTTE guerrilla fighters not designated as suicide bombers, LTTE members carry cyanide capsules around their necks, which they are expected to swallow rather than be captured by Sri Lankan security forces. Although we discussed the fact that women have worked as propagandists for the LTTE, mothers, wives, sisters, and cousins also fulfill the roles of historical conscience in that society and contribute to a culture and glorification of martyrdom.

Finally, other nonviolent organizations can serve as the historical conscience of a society, laying the foundation for support for terrorism, and women similarly can play a role in these organizations. Hizb ut-Tahrir al-Islami (HT), also known as the Islamic Party of Liberation, for example, has used women to recruits new female members. HT is not a terrorist organization. Instead, it is a highly organized, non-violent, grassroots conservative Islamist political movement. HT is interesting nonetheless, especially in the context of women as historical conscience, because it espouses pan-Islam and the restoration of the Khalifa or Caliphate, as does al-Qa'ida.[33] HT contends that women are some of its most effective recruiters for potential new members. In HT, women typically recruit other women for membership and focus especially on the women of an imprisoned member's family.[34]

In sum, this section examined women as historical consciences for terrorist groups and how that relates to the recruitment of new fighters for a wide variety of terrorist groups. This particular role—women as historical consciences—is much less direct than the other roles of women recruiters discussed in this chapter. That is, it is a role that is somewhat vague and difficult to define because it often is unintentional. In many societies, it is traditional for mothers to tell the stories about the difficulties experienced by past generations, and these stories are repeated generation after generation. It is seemingly innocuous. Nonetheless, women as historical consciences tend to reinforce enmity between communities, making the peace process more difficult or even laying the foundation for the motivations and beliefs for future recruits. For this reason we have chosen to categorize this role as "women as recruiters."

CONCLUSION

Both terrorist and insurgent groups reach out to support populations in order to bring new members into their organizations. Indeed, the ability to replenish logisticians, fundraisers, suicide bombers, guerrilla fighters, and even terrorist leadership is essential to the success and survival of a clandestine group. Two basic patterns of recruitment exist. First, family members and friends often encourage potential recruits to join a terrorist or insurgent group. In this sense, close relationships serve as the vehicle for individuals to eventually join terrorist groups and participate in violent activities. Our analysis of twenty-two different terrorist and insurgent groups for this study suggests that women often function as recruiters in this way. In particular, women sometimes function as the historical conscience of their society and, as such, mothers, sisters, wives, and cousins knowingly or unknowingly encourage their family members to become terrorists. Women as historical conscience, in this regard, became strikingly clear in societies with long-term conflict, such as Northern Ireland or Sri Lanka. Similarly, examples exist of women providing an essential link between friends and militant groups and functioning as facilitators for these terrorist and insurgent groups. We found examples of this "friends as facilitators," particularly in the Palestinian territories.

Second, another general pattern of recruitment into terrorist and insurgent groups also exists. Sometimes, militant groups use recruiters to reach out and identify individuals with certain characteristics and skills to bring into the terrorist or insurgent group. This reaching out can be coercive or benign, and we found examples of women conducting both forms of recruitment in our research. Interestingly, coercive measures appear to have been utilized by women recruiters for groups under significant pressure by counterterrorism and counterinsurgency authorities. Examples, in this regard, include the FARC and the Shining Path.

Finally, it is worth stressing that in some circumstances women have taken it upon themselves to be recruiters despite reluctance by terrorist leaders to utilize them in this way. We found this pattern to be particularly true for al-Qa'ida and other associated terrorist groups. Interestingly, technology appears to have made the difference. That is, technology allowed women supporters of al-Qa'ida to engage as propagandists from their homes in Europe and the Middle East without being directly accountable to al-Qa'ida leaders. So it is arguable that technology has empowered women to become more heavily involved in the recruitment of future terrorists, including logisticians, fundraisers, suicide bombers, and guerrilla fighters. We expect this pattern to continue in the future.

4

Women as Suicide Bombers

Although women typically play the role of logistician in terrorist groups, they also have fought and died for their causes. In fact, in our study of twenty-two different terrorist and insurgent groups, eight have utilized women as suicide operatives or martyrs. Scholars often have been puzzled at what might motivate individuals to become suicide bombers. This puzzlement is only amplified when it comes to women operatives. In many instances, a certain mystique has emerged around women terrorists. They are seen on the one hand as more deadly and more determined than their male counterparts, but oddly enough also as tragic romantic characters.

For example, the Chechen women suicide bombers have horrified observers worldwide with their seemingly callous devotion to the Chechen cause, prompting the name Black Widows. It is an excellent name, evoking both deadliness and some degree of tragedy. Indeed, to some, the only logical explanation for these women's devotion is that their husbands and lovers must have been killed by Russian security forces. This mystique, however, is somewhat misplaced, because female operatives are motivated by a complex variety of factors, just as their male counterparts.[1]

Nevertheless, sometimes women suicide bombers evidence different life experiences and therefore motivations different from men. Thenmuli Rajaratnam, for example, was a suicide bomber for the Liberation Tigers of Tamil Eelam (LTTE) in Sri Lanka. On 21 May 1991, she assassinated former Prime Minister of India Rajiv Gandhi. Gandhi had been campaigning for the Congress Party and left his motorcade to walk along the road and greet his supporters. Thenmuli Rajaratnam approached him with a garland, handed Gandhi the gift, bent down to touch his feet in respect, and then detonated a suicide belt hidden beneath her clothes. According to LTTE lore, Thenmuli Rajaratnam was persuaded to become a suicide bomber because of tragic life-changing events. All four of her brothers reportedly were killed by Indian security forces in a raid of her village and more importantly, she was gang-raped in that same raid. Of course, some experts dispute this story as LTTE rhetoric, but regardless of its truth the story clearly holds power within the Tamil community, both male and female, evoking some expectation that women are motivated more frequently than not by strong personal experiences, rather than mere political objectives.[2]

Wafa Idris's story presents a different perspective. She was the first female suicide bomber in the Palestinian territories during the al-Aqsa Intifada, which occurred between September 2000 and July 2003. Wafa Idris resided in the Amari Refugee Camp near Ramallah and did not associate with any of the Palestinian terrorist groups or youth activist groups prior to her attack. In fact, she volunteered for the Red Crescent, working as a nurse in ambulances. She approached the al-Aqsa Martyrs' Brigades, however, in 2002 and volunteered herself as a suicide bomber for the terrorist group. The al-Aqsa Martyrs' Brigades functioned as a militant off-shoot of former President Yasser Arafat's Fatah, during the al-Aqsa Intifada. As such, the al-Aqsa Martyrs' Brigades was a secularist-nationalist terrorist group that often competed with Hamas (Harakat al-Muqawama al-Islamiyya) for recruits and credibility. Upon joining al-Aqsa Martyrs' Brigades, Wafa Idris subsequently detonated a 10 kg rucksack filled with explosives in downtown Jerusalem, on Jaffa Road.[3]

Two different explanations have been given for Wafa Idris's decision to approach al-Aqsa Martyrs' Brigades and volunteer to become a suicide bomber. To some, Wafa Idris was motivated presumably by her reduced status in Palestinian society after her divorce from her husband. According to this logic, Wafa Idris's only option would be to volunteer as a suicide bomber; thus, her motivations would have been similar to Thenmuli Rajaratnam.[4] Alternatively, others have argued that Wafa Idris had been shot three times by Israeli forces while riding in an ambulance. These experiences, coupled with day-to-day difficulties under Israeli occupation, arguably prompted sheer anger and frustration at the daily lives of Palestinians in the mind of Wafa Idris and eventually resulted in her decision to become a suicide bomber.[5] In either explanation Wafa Idris's motivations come across as less tragic than Thenmuli Rajaratnam, almost presenting Idris as a somewhat naïve female heroine.

These examples illustrate the diversity of women suicide bombers in the terrorism community, not even considering women as logisticians, recruiters, vanguards, or even guerrilla fighters. Women have played this role in nationalist-separatist groups (LTTE in Sri Lanka and the al-Aqsa Martyrs' Brigades in the Palestinian territories), religious extremist groups (al-Qa'ida in Iraq, or AQI), and Marxist–Leninist groups

(Partiya Karkerên Kurdistan or PKK in Turkey). Some are motivated by deep personal grievances and others by political objectives, while yet others become used to the life of a combat veteran and do not know how to reassimilate into everyday life. Indeed, this diversity is somewhat striking and calls into question past assumptions about women terrorists. This chapter addresses the role of women as suicide bombers, examining both their motivations and how terrorist groups choose to deploy these lethal weapons. We conclude that for the most part, women suicide bombers evidence the same motivations as men. The main difference, therefore, is not in the minds of women bombers, but in the minds of the leaders of their respective terrorist organizations.

MOTIVATIONS

On 11 September 2001, nineteen al-Qa'ida operatives essentially turned themselves into suicide bombers as they flew airplanes into New York City's World Trade Center and the Department of Defense's Pentagon building in the Washington, D.C., metro area. Since that time, more and more scholars have attempted to explore why individuals become suicide bombers as part of terrorist groups. Are suicide bombers mostly motivated by religious extremism? What about poverty? Are less-educated individuals more susceptible to recruitment? Is the choice ultimately rational or irrational? Although most of the research on this topic has related to men, it is worth contextualizing the role of female suicide bombers in the broader academic understanding of suicide terrorism in general.

For example, Mohammad Atta was one of the key operational planners and leaders for the 11 September 2001 attacks. He came from an apparently middle-class Egyptian family and moved to Germany at the age of twenty-four to study urban planning. In Germany, Mohammad Atta and several friends came to know an al-Qa'ida recruiter, Mohammad Hayder Zammar, eventually forming the Hamburg Cell. The Hamburg Cell provided operational and logistical support to the September 2001 attacks.[6] The case of Mohammad Atta is interesting because he did not come from an impoverished family, nor were his parents religious extremists by all accounts. Interviews with friends and acquaintances suggest that Mohammad Atta was motivated primarily by perceived injustices faced by Muslims worldwide.[7] Yet questions still remain as to what factors truly motivated his membership in the Hamburg Cell as well as his eventual participation in the September 2001 attacks. These questions on Mohammad Atta's motivations essentially parallel academic studies on terrorist motivations. That is, experts have attempted to delineate the degree to which a variety of factors, including age, education, economic status, religious beliefs, mentors, other friendships, and tragic life events have affected individuals' choices to become suicide bombers.

Since 11 September 2001, religious extremism has been viewed as one of the likely motivating factors for suicide bombers. In particular, commentary of this nature tends to focus on Salafism or a form of Sunni Islam espoused by al-Qa'ida. Salafists advocate for a return to Islamic beliefs and practices from the time of the Prophet Mohammad and look to reestablish a Caliphate in the Muslim world. Of course, not all Salafists are terrorists, but some believe that violent jihad should be used to pursue this new Caliphate. Thus, it is logical to assume that religious extremism plays a role in motivating suicide bombers.

Beyond religious rhetoric, al-Qa'ida media—including the as-Sahab Web site and underground DVDs—promote violent jihad as a religious duty for every Muslim, and testimony provided by some former jihadists suggests that this perception of jihad as a religious duty has some resonance. Abdullah Anas, for example, fought against Soviet forces in Afghanistan during the early to mid-1980s. An Algerian, Abdullah Anas was a member of Maktab al-Khidamat, Abdullah Azzam and Osama bin Laden's precursor to al-Qa'ida. In his autobiography, Abdullah Anas testified that this argument helped influence his decision to travel to Afghanistan and fight.[8] Similarly, some commentators have argued that the public denunciation of suicide bombing tactics by noted Islamic philosophers and even former jihadists have helped stem the tide of new recruits into al-Qa'ida.[9] If true, this trend suggests that religious arguments must play at least some role in motivating suicide bombers.

In contrast, in his book *Dying to Win*, Robert Pape examined 315 suicide attacks and concluded that more bombers came from countries that do not exhibit popular sympathy for religious extremism than those with broad popular support for religious extremism.[10] Robert Pape's work, therefore, provided some alternative explanations to religious extremism as a motivating factor for suicide terrorism. Similarly, Stephen Holmes, contributing a chapter to the book *Making Sense of Suicide Missions*, has argued that religious practices themselves, more than the specific beliefs, help sustain individuals' commitment to suicide terrorism.[11] In this sense, Holmes believes that it is the ritual activities associated with recruitment and indoctrination that prompt individuals to become suicide bombers, rather than somewhat irrational worldviews, desperation, or even a particular religion.

This viewpoint was confirmed by a study conducted by the Singapore government on Jemaah Islamiyya (JI). JI is a terrorist group operating primarily in southeast Asia, with ties to individuals in Malaysia,

Singapore, Indonesia, Thailand, and the Philippines. It was responsible for the October 2002 Bali bombing as well as the 2003 attack against the Marriott hotel in Jakarta. The Singapore government arrested and interrogated thirty-one JI activists in December 2001, attempting to identity their motivations for becoming terrorists.[12] The study of these individuals determined that they were highly intelligent and held respectable jobs. One of the key findings from that study was that shared religious values combined with feelings of fraternity moved individuals through a radicalization process. In this process, the feelings of fraternity were reinforced by ritualistic practices, such as code names and pledges of allegiance.[13]

Although academics and policymakers alike still have a number of unanswered questions on terrorists' motivations to become suicide bombers, consensus has been reached on some factors. Suicide bombers are not irrational actors. They are motivated by a variety of factors: some demographics (e.g., age), but mostly psychographics (e.g., beliefs). Individuals are often prompted to consider the possibility of becoming a suicide bomber by perceived injustices, but they almost always radicalize at a young age and as part of a peer group, rather than independently.[14] Indeed, individuals more often than not progress through a radicalization trajectory that allows them to move from considering the possibility to being committed to their decision.

Increasingly, women too have emerged as suicide bombers in areas of conflict, such as Sri Lanka, Turkey and Chechnya, and the West Bank and Gaza Strip, as well as Iraq. The question then arises: are women motivated to become suicide bombers by the same factors as men? That is, are women also motivated by perceived injustices and solidarity with a peer group, or do other factors weigh more heavily in their decision-making processes? Most literature from women's studies would suggest that women experience life differently from men and thus are likely to be motivated differently as well. Yet very few studies appear to address these questions with regard to women suicide bombers, and so the answers are somewhat unclear.

Some of the perhaps most infamous female suicide bombers are the Chechen Black Widows. Chechen separatists have fought against the presence of Russian security forces in an effort to establish a separate Chechnya state or at least an autonomous governing structure. On 7 June 2000 the first female Chechen suicide bombers, Khava Barayeva and Luisa Magomadova, crashed a truck full of explosives into a Russian security forces building in Chechnya, killing two and wounding an additional five people. Indeed, Chechen women were involved in twenty-two of twenty-seven suicide attacks between 2000 and 2006, with a total of forty-seven female suicide bombers.[15]

Of course, of those forty-seven women, nineteen were involved in one particular attack: the October 2002 hostage situation at the Dubrovka Theater in Moscow.[16] In this terrorist attack, approximately forty Chechen rebels took control of the theater and held more than 800 people hostage. They demanded Russian withdrawal from Chechnya as a condition for the release of these hostages. Russian security forces eventually raided the theater, killing thirty-nine terrorists and injuring more than 200 hostages. The Dubrovka Theater incident is significant because all nineteen women operatives reportedly wore suicide belts, whereas their male counterparts did not. This difference has caused some speculation that perhaps the women had been coerced (e.g., raped and drugged) into participation.

Nevertheless, most evidence suggests that Black Widows were not coerced. For example, scholars Anne Speckhard and Khapta Akhmedova interviewed the family and relatives of Chechen suicide bombers for their article, "The Making of a Martyr." As part of that research, they interviewed the friend of one of the women involved in the Dubrovka Theater attack. This woman had apparently attempted to loan her friend, the forthcoming suicide bomber, money but was refused; she subsequently found a note explaining this refusal:

> I could not tell you the truth. And I could not take money from you because I could not go to paradise with unpaid debts. I know that many people will not understand us, and will make accusations. But I believe that you will understand all. Do not trust anything that will be said about us. They will say that we bargained and demanded dollars and a plane in exchange for the hostages. It's not the truth. We go on jihad. We know that all of us will die. We are ready for it. We will not bargain and we will stand to the end. Forgive me if there is anything I have done to hurt you. I do not say goodbye. I know that we shall meet in heaven. Comfort my mother. She will suffer very much, she never understood me. Tell her that I myself wanted it. I am happy that I have deserved jihad.[17]

Nothing in this note suggests that male Chechen fighters coerced this woman into becoming a suicide bomber. It appears that she was willing to die, while at the same time she was concerned for the pain she might cause loved ones at her sacrifice. In subsequent work, Speckhard and Akhmedova concluded that Chechen women were motivated by the same factors as male suicide bombers, that is, perceived injustices and personal grievances. Additionally, family and associates observed changes in the Chechen operatives' behavior immediately following some personal grievance, primarily the loss of a loved one. These changes in behavior included depression, social alienation, and isolation, aggression, and calls for revenge.[18]

In addition to the Black Widows associated with the Chechen rebels, Palestinian women suicide bombers have garnered significant attention in the international media. Women have traditionally played the role of logistician in the Palestinian national movement. So the emergence of Palestinian women operatives during the al-Aqsa Intifada raised eyebrows in the counterterrorism expert community. Some studies have suggested that Palestinian terrorist leaders were reluctant to allow women to sacrifice themselves in this way, perhaps indicating desperation on the part of terrorist groups for new recruits, whereas other experts have interpreted the presence of female suicide bombers from the Palestinian territories as a natural step in that society's feminist movement. Either way, the motivations of these Palestinian women present a useful point of comparison for the Chechen women operatives.

According to a study by Yoram Schweitzer, between January 2002 and May 2006 sixty-seven women attempted to carry out suicide bombings in Israel, with eight actually being successful.[19] These eight women operatives are listed below:

- 27 January 2002: Wafa Idris, age twenty-eight, was the first female suicide bomber from the Palestinian territories. She detonated her 10-kg rucksack filled with explosives in downtown Jerusalem, on Jaffa Road. Prior to that attack, Wafa had been a volunteer at the Palestinian Red Crescent in Ramallah. She was affiliated with the al-Aqsa Martyrs' Brigades.
- 27 February 2002: Dareen Abu Aysheh, age twenty-one, was a student at al-Najah University in Nablus. She was affiliated with the al-Aqsa Martyrs' Brigade. Her male cousin had blown himself up in Tel Aviv seventeen months previously.
- 29 March 2002: Ayat Akhras, age eighteen, successfully detonated a suicide device outside a supermarket in Jerusalem. Ayat came from the Deheisha refugee camp and had recently lost a close male relative. She also was engaged. Ayat was affiliated with the al-Aqsa Martyrs' Brigade.
- 12 April 2002: Andaleeb Takafka, age twenty, from a Palestinian town near Bethlehem, conducted a suicide attack in a pedestrian mall in central Jerusalem. She was affiliated with the al-Aqsa Martyrs' Brigades.
- 19 May 2003: Hiba Daraghmah, age nineteen, blew herself up outside a shopping mall in Afula. Both Islamic Jihad and al-Aqsa Martyrs' Brigades claimed that Hiba was a member of their organization. She was an English literature student at al Quds University in Jenin and reportedly was devoted to her family, but had been raped at the age of fourteen.

- 4 October 2003: Hanadi Tayseer Jaradat, age twenty-nine, was an apprentice real estate attorney whose younger brother had been killed by security forces. She detonated her suicide belt at the Maxim restaurant in Haifa.
- 14 January 2004: Reem Salih al-Rayasha, age twenty-one, came from a wealthy family and had two children. She was the first female suicide bomber associated with Hamas and, allegedly, was having an affair with a married man. Reem wrapped the suicide device around her leg and told soldiers at the checkpoint that she had metal in her leg from surgery.
- 22 September 2004: Zayneb Abu Salem, age eighteen, blew herself up at a police checkpoint in Jerusalem. She was from the Askar refugee camp in Nablus and affiliated with the al-Aqsa Martyrs' Brigades. She was the eighth female suicide bomber and reportedly the forty-first recruited by terror organizations.[20]

In his review of all sixty-seven women, Schweitzer found that most were unmarried and young and had an above-average education. This basic profile parallels findings from studies of male suicide bombers in the Palestinian territories. Additionally, 44 percent of the female suicide bombers were associated with secularist-nationalist terrorist groups, including Fatah's al-Aqsa Martyrs' Brigades and the Popular Front for the Liberation of Palestine, while only 9 percent were associated with religious terrorist groups, such as Hamas and the Palestinian Islamic Jihad.[21] According to data on suicide attacks during the al-Aqsa Intifada, a majority were conducted by secularist-nationalist groups, rather than religious terrorist groups. Nonetheless, the disproportion of female suicide bombers for secularist-nationalist versus religious terrorist groups far exceeds the numbers themselves, suggesting that secularist-nationalists were more willing to utilize women than the religious terrorist groups in the Palestinian territories.

Like Anne Speckhard and Khapta Akhmedova's study of Chechen women operatives, Schweitzer attempted to interview the family, friends, and captured women operatives themselves. It is clear from his account of these interviews that Palestinian women were motivated by a collection of personal grievances and perceived injustices from the Israeli occupation, very similar to the conclusions of Speckhard and Akhmedova. Schweitzer, for example, presented the following statement by one captured female suicide bomber:

> The goal of my going on the mission was not vengeance; it was to deliver a message to people in Israel to stop the occupation, and to make them feel the pain that the Palestinians felt. We tried to stop our suffering many

times, in various ways, but no one listened to us. As a Palestinian girl, how can I stop the suffering if my home is constantly under occupation, and there are tanks surrounding my home, while everyone in the world is enjoying music, and the only melody I can hear is the sound of bullets. Had I carried out my mission, I would have made Israeli society think twice about why I had blown myself up. The Israelis who voted for Sharon [former Israeli Prime Minister Ariel Sharon] are to blame for the situation that has been created.[22]

On the basis of this statement and the one provided above from a Chechen female operative, one could conclude that women suicide bombers essentially are motivated by factors very similar to those of male suicide bombers: perceived injustices. It is also interesting to note that even a majority of the female suicide bombers in the Palestinian territories are members of secularist-nationalist terrorist groups, not religious terrorist groups, contradicting the most common perception of suicide attacks in the Middle East.

Finally, the conflict in Iraq witnessed an upsurge in attacks by female suicide bombers in 2007 and 2008. Between 2003 and 2008, approximately forty-five women conducted suicide attacks against U.S. forces and civilians in Iraq: more than thirty took place in 2007 and 2008.[23] Most of these attacks occurred in Diyala Province and are attributed to AQI, despite Ayman al-Zawahiri's statement in January 2008 that al-Qa'ida does not utilize women fighters. Moreover, Iraqi and U.S. authorities have stated that although women suicide bombers appear to be younger than their male counterparts in Iraq, they are more highly educated.[24] So, interestingly, the pattern of female suicide bombers in Iraq parallels that of the Palestinian territories in this regard.

One of the most interesting examples of female suicide bombers in Iraq is the case of a Belgian woman named Muriel Degauque. Between 2003 and 2008 in Iraq, suicide bombers in general fell into two different categories. The first category was Iraqi suicide bombers. That is, individuals born in Iraq who decided to join with al-Qa'ida to conduct suicide attacks against U.S. forces and other civilian targets. The second category of suicide bombers was "foreign fighters," or individuals from other countries, primarily in the Middle East, who came to Iraq to fight against the United States and its allies. In the entire population of suicide attacks in Iraq between 2003 and 2008, foreign fighters conducted the vast majority of these attacks and indigenous Iraqi bombers represented a minority of the bombers. This pattern was not true for women suicide bombers: most were Iraqis. So Muriel's story is somewhat atypical of female suicide bombers in Iraq, but is intriguing nonetheless.

Muriel was a resident of Belgium who worked in a bakery and was born into the Catholic faith. She initially converted to Islam after her first marriage to an older Turkish man, but that marriage ended in divorce. At the time, most of her neighbors assumed that Muriel married her first husband so that he could obtain citizenship in Belgium. Muriel's second husband was a man of Algerian origin who also lived in Belgium. Subsequent to this marriage, Muriel moved with her new husband to Morocco apparently to study Islam. In Morocco, Muriel donned a veil and increasingly adopted strict Muslim practices, while her husband—according to authorities—was recruited by al-Qa'ida members.[25] Soon thereafter, Muriel and her husband returned to Belgium, but she distanced herself from her Catholic family.[26] Indeed, Muriel and her husband were not the only al-Qa'ida recruits in Belgium at the time, as European authorities eventually arrested fourteen individuals on terrorism charges who were identified as part of al-Qa'ida's Belgium network. Still, at the age of thirty-eight, Muriel traveled to Iraq with her husband via Turkey and Syria with the intention of joining al-Qa'ida in that country.[27] On 9 November 2005, Muriel detonated her suicide vest near a U.S. military patrol in Baquba, wounding one soldier. Her husband was killed in a U.S. military raid the next day; he also had planned to conduct a suicide attack. Although this story is atypical, European authorities have expressed concern that women converts to Islam in Western countries might be particularly susceptible to al-Qa'ida recruits.

Other examples exist of Iraqi female suicide bombers. In June 2008, *Time* published a story about Hasna Maryi, an Iraqi female suicide bomber who conducted an attack against an Iraqi police checkpoint in 2007, killing three policemen and injuring approximately ten civilians. In this attack, Hasna walked up to the checkpoint and seemed to trip, calling out for help. When the policemen rushed to her, Hasna detonated the suicide vest. According to her family, Hasna was not particularly religious or impoverished, nor was she raped or abused prior to this suicide attack. Instead, Hasna helped her brother prepare for a suicide mission, and when that mission was unsuccessful, volunteered herself to try. Al-Qa'ida members reportedly provided Hasna's family with two DVDs. The first DVD was a recording made by Hasna prior to her suicide attack, in which she indicated that her brother's death was the primary motivating factor for her choice. The second DVD was a recording of the attack itself: as Hasna detonated her suicide belt, the cameraman was recorded as saying, "God is great.... The stupid woman did it."[28]

Despite this statement, it is clear from studies of female suicide bombers that for the most part they are not stupid or ignorant. In fact, they appear to be more highly educated than their male counterparts.

Women operatives also progress toward violence, sometimes as part of a peer group, but almost always in parallel with their male counterparts. If any difference emerges between men and women, it appears that Chechen, Palestinian, and Iraqi women suicide bombers perhaps emphasize personal grievances versus perceived injustices more than men as motivation for why they chose to become a suicide operative. That is, media interviews and academic studies of women suicide bombers tend to record statements by female suicide bombers that reflect personal grievances as bases for motivation, in addition to other factors, as compared to similar studies of male suicide bombers. It is possible that these differences in articulated motivations are truly significant or they could simply be a sign of the types of questions asked by interviewers or even the role that women play in those societies in general. However, at the very least, it suggests some interesting similarities and differences between the motivations of male and female suicide bombers.

DEPLOYMENT

If uncertainty exists as to the motivations of female suicide bombers, especially as compared to male suicide bombers, it also remains unclear as to whether or not women suicide bombers are deployed in the same way as men by terrorist leaders. Returning to the aforementioned study by Robert Pape, his research into suicide terrorism in general suggests that terrorist groups use suicide bombers to attack strategic targets, or in other words, targets that they might not be able to hit successfully otherwise.[29] Statements by terrorist leaders themselves reinforce this finding.

For example, Abdel Aziz Rantisi, the second in command of Hamas during the second Intifada and successor to Hamas founder Sheikh Yasin after his assassination in 2004, was asked about the utility of suicide attacks in May 2002. He replied as follows:

> In killing our civilians, our kids, Israel has used F-16s, Apache helicopters, missiles, tanks, they even demolished houses burying people alive in Jenin. So, if we had weapons like F-16s and Apaches, we would use them, but we haven't, and so we are left with two choices. Either we surrender and accept a quiet death, or we defend ourselves using our own means of struggle. And one of our most effective means, which can rival the impact of their F-16s, is martyr operations.[30]

Despite the fact that Hamas is well known for its use of suicide bombers, however, most evidence suggests that Hamas leaders never chose to deploy female suicide bombers, regardless of the desperate state of their conflict with Israel. This hesitation indicates that perhaps terrorist leaders consider the decision to deploy women suicide bombers differently, or they calculate the decision differently, than that of their male counterparts.

Close examination of other terrorist groups reveals similar patterns. On 30 June 1996 the first female suicide bomber associated with the PKK (or Kurdish Workers' Party) in Turkey killed six soldiers and wounded an additional thirty. Like the Chechen separatists, the PKK has fought to establish a Kurdish nation-state, comprised of territory from Turkey, Iraq, and Iran. The first PKK female suicide bomber had a suicide bombing belt strapped to her stomach and built in such a way to suggest that she was pregnant. In fact, PKK women operatives have conducted eleven of a total of fifteen suicide bombings in Turkey, and three of these women wore belts that made them look pregnant.[31] According to a study by Israeli counterterrorism expert Ehud Sprinzak, the PKK specifically has utilized women operatives as suicide bombers because they are better able to slip past Turkish security measures.[32] At first blush, this explanation suggests that terrorist leaders' rationale for the use of female suicide bombers parallels their rationale for the tactic in general: it provides a greater rate of success.

Yet other evidence suggests that PKK leaders have thought through the potential costs and benefits of the deployment of female suicide bombers versus their male counterparts. For example, the PKK has used women operatives disproportionately as suicide bombers. This terrorist group reportedly has 5,000 militants with 1,100 women operatives, or 22 percent, whereas 73 percent of its suicide bombers have been women.[33] Other studies of the role of women in the PKK similarly suggest that its leaders have struggled with the best way to incorporate women fighters into the overall organizational structure. For example, Dr. Nihat Ali Özcan has observed that the PKK initially paired women fighters with male counterparts in guerrilla operations, perhaps to better guarantee success.[34] This approach exposed the women to sexual harassment, and even though these incidents were punished, PKK leaders had to rethink their approach. To avoid future sexual harassment, the PKK determined to separate female and male operatives. This separation, however, exposed the women operatives to criticisms of not being as determined or as aggressive as the men. Naturally, the PKK women operatives wanted to prove themselves as committed as the male operatives, and attempting to do so, according to Dr. Nihat Ali Özcan, volunteered for suicide operations.[35]

This story of the PKK in Turkey and its internal struggles reveals a more general difficulty in understanding terrorist decision making.

Sometimes terrorist groups make decisions based on how they can best achieve their overarching strategy, but at other times terrorist leaders are required to deviate from that path to resolve internal strife. It appears that PKK women operatives initially came to be used as suicide bombers because of their desire to prove themselves as committed as the men in their organization, but PKK leaders quickly realized the operational value of women operatives and so continued to deploy them as suicide bombers.

Similar patterns exist within the LTTE in Sri Lanka and its use of women suicide operatives. Like the PKK, the LTTE has fought to create a separate autonomous Tamil region in Sri Lanka. In pursuit of this objective, as of July 2006, the LTTE had deployed a total of 177 suicide bombers, and sixty-five of them were women.[36] As with the PKK, women operatives appear to be disproportionately deployed as suicide bombers in the LTTE. For example, according to the LTTE Web site, it has 14,000 operatives, and 4,000 of them are women, comprising 29 percent. Yet 36 percent of all suicide bombings have been conducted by LTTE women.[37] Interviews with Sri Lankan security officials likewise have revealed that female Black Tigers are separated from their male counterparts, and relationships are not allowed to develop between them. This separation suggests that LTTE leaders, like those of the PKK, are worried about issues of sexual harassment or abuse. Additionally, it also is possible that LTTE leaders do not want relationships to develop between male and female suicide bombers, given their forthcoming missions.

Likewise, AQI has received some criticism from within the wider al-Qa'ida movement for its use of female suicide bombers. Most newspaper articles suggest that the emergence of female suicide bombers in Iraq represents a deliberate tactical shift on behalf of AQI. The incentives for AQI to recruit females as suicide bombers are manifold. Most bombers don abayas, easily concealing the suicide vest underneath. In addition, because Iraqi culture inhibits male security forces from searching the women, they often are able to slip through checkpoints. As one frustrated U.S. soldier put it, "[i]f we are told by our superiors not to look at a woman because Arab culture tells us not to, then how are we supposed to suspect them?"[38] In this sense, the experiences of U.S. soldiers in Iraq parallel the experiences of French soldiers in Algeria during the 1950s. Recall from Chapter 2 that the Groupe Islamique Arme in Algeria utilized women as decoys for the Millennium bombing plot because they could more easily slip through security checkpoints. The same trend has emerged in Iraq, although with the adaptation of women being the suicide bombers themselves, rather than just couriers.

Notably, the choice to use women doubles AQI's recruitment pool. A wide recruitment pool is an especially important advantage given the losses AQI absorbed in al-Anbar province with the emergence of the tribal awakening councils in 2007 and 2008. In fact, some commentators have pointed to the idea that the recruitment of female suicide bombers is a sign of weakness in AQI.[39] Because AQI has been marginalized in al-Anbar province, its leaders have been forced to adapt and adjust both geographically (to Diyala) and tactically (by recruiting women).

Lastly, it is worth noting that the stance of Ayman al-Zawahri on female participation in al-Qa'ida operations has been challenged. Yusuf al-Qaradawi, an influential Egyptian scholar, issued a 2003 fatwa sanctioning female suicide bombings.[40] Al-Qaradawi argued that "when the enemy assaults a given Muslim territory, it becomes incumbent upon all its residents to fight against them to the extent that a woman should go out even without the consent of her husband."[41] In short, for both pragmatic reasons and philosophical ones, AQI's view of the role of women in suicide bombing campaigns has changed.

In sum, there appears to be a historical progression in how terrorist leaders have deployed female suicide bombers. Initially, it appears that terrorist leaders have used women in response to pressure by counterterrorism authorities. Either women were utilized because they could more easily avoid scrutiny or because male recruits were in short supply. Perhaps terrorist leaders intended to deploy female operatives only for a short time, until they could recover from the pressure placed on them by counterterrorism authorities. Perhaps not. But it appears that once terrorist leaders deployed women, it was almost impossible for them to retract, and this successful tactic took on a life of its own. Moreover, the use of female suicide bombers in most cases drew external criticism and caused internal strife, and so terrorist leaders had to weigh the tactical benefits against this criticism and strife.

CONCLUSION

If having women in the ranks of operatives really causes that much trouble, why not simply use them as recruiters and logisticians? It must be easier, organizationally, to separate women logisticians from male operatives. Yet the Turkish PKK, Tamil LTTE, Palestinian al-Aqsa Martyrs' Brigades, Chechen separatists, and Iraqi AQI have repeatedly deployed women as suicide bombers; indeed, sometimes disproportionately to men. This pattern suggests two possible explanations: either the operational benefit of women operatives out-weighs the internal and external strife that they bring to the organization, or they are held as less valuable than their male counterparts. The latter explanation is less persuasive. Primarily, the LTTE is known to use its most trustworthy, battle-proven cadre as suicide operatives, not expendable individuals. It therefore seems more likely that from the perspective of the terrorist group, women operatives are actually more valuable than men.

But what about terrorist groups that use suicide bombings as a tactic, but do not deploy female suicide bombers? Significantly, some of the terrorist groups most commonly associated with suicide terrorism do not used women operatives. Hizballah, for example, conducted a number of suicide operations between 1982 and 1995, but none of the operatives were women. Hamas, too, has been reluctant to use female suicide bombers. The one exception was Reem Salih al-Rayasha, who was married to a Hamas operative and apparently had an affair with a married man.[42] JI in Southeast Asia has never used women as suicide operatives, nor has the senior leadership of al-Qa'ida. Indeed, the absence of suicide bombers from these groups, while other terrorist groups have demonstrated their operational value, suggests strong barriers to the use of women as suicide bombers. Some terrorist groups clearly have been able to overcome these barriers, while others have not.

5

Women as Operational Leaders and Fighters

Up to this point, our book has discussed a wide variety of roles that women have played in terrorist organizations: couriers, decoys, recruiters, propagandists, and even suicide bombers. In most of these situations, the day-to-day activities of women in their respective terrorist and insurgent groups have been dictated by predominantly male operational leaders, but women also have taken on the responsibility of leading skirmishes with government security forces so that their respective terrorist and insurgent groups can capture and control territory. Beyond skirmishes, women have participated in and led high-profile terrorist attacks against their adversaries. In these instances, women have gone beyond the movement of weapons, fundraising, or even detonating suicide vests. These women have been the leaders and planners for their operations and, as such, merit further discussion.

For example, Eliana Gonzalez was one of five women to join the Revolutionary Armed Forces of Colombia (FARC) in the 1970s. The FARC is a Marxist–Leninist insurgent group that controls territory in southwestern Colombia. Since the 1990s, the FARC also has been heavily involved in drug trafficking. Eliana Gonzalez was eighteen years old when she joined the FARC, leaving behind a husband and daughter. As of 2006, Eliana commanded a FARC unit. According to some accounts, Eliana Gonzalez joined the FARC after the death of her mother and to escape an oppressive farm life. Other stories suggest that her father, apparently, lauded and romanticized FARC leader Manuel Marulanda, "Sure Shot," which contributed to Eliana Gonzalez's decision. She remained with the FARC for more than thirty years, watching her daughter join and a younger son be killed by paramilitaries in retaliation for her membership.[1] In contrast to the tragedy of Thenmuli Rajaratnam or the naïveté of Wafa Idris, two suicide bombers from our previous chapter, therefore, Eliana Gonzalez's image is that of a hardened warrior who probably would accept no other life.

Dora Maria Telles Arguello represents another interesting example of a woman guerrilla fighter in Latin America. Telles was a medical student when she became involved in the Sandinista National Liberation Front, who fought to overthrow Nicaragua's dictator, Anastasio Somoza, in the 1970s. In fact, according to some estimates, approximately 30 percent of the Sandinista guerrilla fighters by the late 1970s were women. Many of them had been recruited as fighters through the Association of Women Confronting the National Problem, which provided aid to women and children victims of the Somoza dictatorship.[2] As a commandante with the Sandinistas, Telles helped Eden Pastora lead an assault against the National Palace in 1978. In this assault, twenty-four Sandinistas dressed as members of the National Guard forced their way into the Palace. Once inside, the Sandinistas killed twenty-three individuals and, under the threat of additional deaths, took approximately 2,000 government officials hostage. The Sandinistas demanded the following: (1) the release of fifty-nine high-profile political prisoners; (2) US$10 million; (3) broadcast of a Sandinista communiqué over the radio; and (4) safe passage out of the country.[3] For the most part Somoza acquiesced to these demands. Telles then went on to lead the Sandinistas' effort in the battle for Leon with three other women commanders. After the Sandinistas' victory, Telles eventually became a Minster of Health under the first Sandinista administration in Nicaragua, as well as a noted historian on Latin America.

Finally, Adriana Faranda was an operational leader for the Italian Red Brigades (RB) during the 1970s. In May 1979, Adriana Faranda along with a dozen other colleagues conducted an assault on the regional headquarters for the Christian Democratic Party. While some of the RB's operatives held guards at gunpoint, others planted timed explosives. The operatives escaped during the chaos after these bombs exploded and subsequently released a communiqué that stated, "The assault on one of the most important and well-guarded structures in the city has shown once again that no place and no person, no matter how well protected, are immune to the sophistication of guerrilla warfare."[4] Adriana Faranda was dedicated to the RB and their revolutionary agenda and, in fact, left a young daughter alone with her family in order to become a full member of the RB, living and functioning clandestinely.[5] She was imprisoned for fourteen years as a result of this and other terrorist attacks conducted in Italy.

These three examples illustrate that women have gone beyond the role of mere tools in the hands of terrorist leaders, taking on leadership positions in the operational cells of terrorist and insurgent groups. Indeed, of the twenty-two different terrorist and insurgent groups in this study, thirteen utilized women as guerrilla fighters or operational leaders. Interestingly, some authors have posited that women are more likely to take on an active fighting role in terrorist and insurgent groups that expouse left-wing agendas, as opposed to ideologically conservative terrorist groups. Daniel E. Georges-Abeyie made this observation in his chapter "Women as Terrorists," in *Perspectives on Terrorism*:

> Various mass-media sources as well as social-control sources, primarily the Federal Bureau of Investigation (FBI) and the International Association of Chiefs of Police (IACP), also concluded that women have played a relatively secondary role in terrorist violence, as well as in terrorist groups, although there have been some notable exceptions. These exceptions are discussed by Russell and Miller, who note that women have occupied an important position in West German terrorist movements, especially in the Baader-Meinhof organization and the Movement Two June where they have constituted one-third of the operational personnel.[6]

In this perspective, left-wing groups are more likely to allow women to fight and take on operational roles as a reflection of societies' expectations of women in general. The Baader-Meinhof Gang (also known as the Red Army Faction), in this context, represents an example of a left-wing group that made room for women operatives in its membership. Gorges-Abeyie would argue that the strong presence of women operatives in the Baader-Meinhof Gang made sense, given the progressive nature of German society in the latter half of the 20th century.

Likewise, the Provisional Irish Republican Army (PIRA) represents another terrorist group that operated in Western society and incorporated women into multiple levels of its organization. In his article "Myths in the Representation of Women Terrorists," Rhiannon Talbot argued:

> For example, women who join the IRA, like the men, are from predominantly working class backgrounds, they are younger than the usual recruiting age around the world, and they often continue to participate after they have had children. Women play a prominent part in all levels of the organization, more so than for the other nationalist revolutionary groups. The IRA in particular is keen to be seen to encourage this participation.[7]

In this article, Talbot appears to be arguing that the PIRA was even more inclusive than the Baader-Meinhof Gang and other left-wing terrorist groups at the time. The historical examples of the Baader-Meinhof terrorist group and the PIRA, therefore, suggest that terrorist groups operating in more progressive societies reflect those societies' values by incorporating women operatives into their organizational structure. In this sense, women terrorists contribute to the terrorist groups' nationalistic or ideological struggle, but they also represent a wider struggle within the society for women's equality.

Contradictory evidence suggests that women have played an important role as operational leaders in other, more culturally conservative, terrorist and insurgent groups as well. These groups include the Partiya Karkerên Kurdistan (PKK), or the Kurdish Workers Party, in Turkey and the Liberation Tigers of Tamil Eelam (LTTE) in Sri Lanka, as well as a variety of Palestinian terrorist groups. This trend suggests that perhaps there is more to learn about the factors that motivate women to become terrorist operatives or the factors that prompt terrorist group leaders to allow women into their inner circles than scholars have previously observed. The following sections explore this dynamic further, beginning with women as guerrilla fighters and then continuing on with a discussion of women as operational leaders.

GUERRILLA FIGHTERS

Guerrilla fighters engage in skirmishes with government security forces in an effort to control people and territory. Although a number of studies have attempted to answer questions as to what motivates suicide bombers, others have explored the motivations of guerrilla fighters, male and female. For example, Professor Alan Krueger from Princeton University further explored the hypothesis that impoverished individuals were more likely to become terrorists in his 2003 article titled "Education, Poverty, and Terrorism: Is There a Causal Connection?"[8] For this study, Krueger examined male Lebanese fighters associated with Hizballah.

Hizballah emerged in the early 1980s in response to the Israeli invasion and occupation of southern Lebanon. Hizballah is perhaps most well known in the United States for its 1983 suicide attack against the U.S. Marine barracks in Beirut, but Hizballah conducted a number of guerrilla attacks against Israeli military convoys and personnel throughout the 1980s and 1990s. We discussed Hizballah slightly in Chapter 2, because it has used women as fundraisers to a limited degree. In his study of terrorist motivations, Krueger attempted to discover to what degree the lack of education and poverty influence individuals' decisions to become Hizballah members. Of the 129 individuals in his dataset, three individuals were suicide bombers, and all were male.[9] Yet it is an interesting starting point for comparison between male and female guerrilla fighters. Indeed, Krueger discovered that Hizballah fighters did not vary in poverty levels from the Lebanese population in general. Moreover, Hizballah fighters were more highly educated than the Lebanese population. Krueger concluded that little evidence suggests that impoverished or poorly educated individuals are disproportionately drawn to become guerrilla fighters.[10] This pattern parallels our findings from Chapter 4 on suicide bombers, both male and female.

Similarly, Albert Bandura explored the "mechanisms of moral disengagement" in his work on terrorist radicalization and recruitment in the 1990s. Bandura posited that individuals typically go through a disengagement process, in which they identify their enemies as less than human. This disengagement process allows individuals to kill their enemies without much remorse.[11] Originally drawn from studies of Nazis, this theory has been applied more recently to individuals who become terrorists.

Past studies on terrorist motivations, therefore, do not appear to reveal any different motivations between those individuals who become suicide bombers and those who become guerrilla fighters. Issues of personal grievance and perceived injustice continue to motivate guerrilla fighters as well as suicide bombers. Like suicide bombers, guerrilla fighters also appear to be relatively intelligent and join terrorist groups with their peers. One might also conclude, based on comparisons between male operatives, that female guerrilla operatives' motivation is similar to that of female suicide bombers. This appears to be true for the most part. Yet, some differences exist. In particular, women operatives, who play the role of guerrilla fighters, tend to emphasize the struggle for the liberation of women in their autobiographies and in interviews more than suicide bombers. That is, women guerrilla fighters appear to see the fight for women's liberation as part of the broader political objectives articulated by terrorist groups.

For example, the Web site for the LTTE in Sri Lanka specifically addresses the heroism of women guerrilla fighters. In fact, Tamil Eelam Women's Day is celebrated on 10 October, which marks the date of the death of the first LTTE woman guerrilla fighter. The LTTE formed its women's wing—referred to as Suthanthirap Paravaikal, or Birds of Freedom—in August 1983 and began to recruit women members at that time.[12] According to most accounts, the women's wing was formed initially to provide Tamil women with the tools of self-defense, apparently against Indian and Singhalese security forces. The Birds of Freedom was also created in an effort to utilize women's voices as rhetorical support for the LTTE.[13] Approximately one year after the formation of the

Birds of Freedom, however, women cadré were rolled into a military unit. LTTE guerrilla fighters even eventually saw combat, beginning in 1986.

Since that time, LTTE women guerrillas have manned checkpoints, guarded defensive bunkers, and played a role in armed combat. They also are involved in logistical tasks, such as ammunition resupply, medical services, and transportation.[14] In March 1993, the leader of the LTTE, Velupillai Pirabaharan, gave a tribute to women guerrilla fighters. His speech was recorded on the LTTE Web site, as follows:

> ... The liberation of women is a liberation within our liberation struggle which is on the ascendance. The ideology of women's liberation is a child born out of the womb of our liberation struggle. The growth and renaissance of the struggle is an unparalleled history by itself. The Tamil EEelam [sic] revolutionary woman has transformed herself as a Tiger for the Liberation of our land and liberation of women.... She, like a fire that burns away injustices, has taken up arms. Our movement paved the way for this historical change.[15]

Of course, Pirabaharan was clearly playing to the crowd of LTTE women in this speech, but it is interesting that he chose to link the concept of women's liberation with national liberation. Indeed, this statement suggests that women's liberation had been connected to national liberation in the minds of female operatives, and LTTE leaders used this connection to reinforce their support and commitment to the terrorist group.

This pattern has emerged in other terrorist groups as well. FARC, for example, has also emphasized the parallels between its organizational goals and the liberation of women. According to the FARC Web site, 35 percent of FARC guerrilla fighters are women, approximately 4,200 of 12,000 fighters. Women operatives have their own name in the FARC, as they do in the LTTE; they are called *guerrillera*. The following commemoration was posted on the FARC Web site:

> The Revolutionary Armed Forces of Colombia–People's Army, FARC-EP, greet all women of the world in commemoration of 8 March, historic date of the ardent struggle for their rights, equality and dignity. Women's rights are also the rights of men and of humanity....
>
> In Colombia, due to the growing popular discontent stemming from social, economic, political, cultural and structural inequalities, complemented by discriminatory treatment towards them, hundreds of women from the countryside and towns are rising up in arms, alongside the men, in the revolutionary struggle, to demand respect for their rights and those of all who are excluded, marginalized, and exploited by the government cast and to demand from the governing system the fulfillment of duties regarding the governed.[16]

As guerrilla fighters, women in the FARC wore the same uniforms as men, carried medium-sized rifles, and were exposed to skirmishes and danger just like the men. Unlike the LTTE, FARC women fighters did not have their own unit, but were scattered throughout the sixty operational "fronts" maintained by FARC.[17] As such, some FARC operatives have fought in rural environments—FARC's stronghold is in the rural southwest of Colombia, but others have taken on responsibilities in urban areas.

For example, Ivon Barragan Tovar was recruited at Colombia's premier National University in Bogota at the age of eighteen or nineteen.[18] According to some accounts, the FARC recruited Tovar because she had street smarts and thus would perform well in an urban environment, something FARC struggled with operationally because it has historical roots in the countryside. Tovar reportedly headed an urban terror cell for the FARC, comprised of five people. Her cell belonged to the Antonio Narino Front, and its primary role was to provide a safe haven for rural operatives as they came into the city.[19] Tovar also taught FARC guerrilla fighters from the countryside how to operate in an urban environment. On 15 October 2003, at the age of twenty-two, Tovar helped with the attempted assassination of Jorge Visbal, the head of the cattlemen's association, covering a FARC comrade while he attempted to escape. She was fatally wounded in the shootout.[20]

The story of Ivon Barragan Tovar presents an interesting contrast to Eliana Gonzalez, who was discussed in the introduction to this chapter. Gonzalez was one of five women to join the FARC in the 1970s and represents one of the most senior-ranking woman, commanding a FARC guerrilla unit in the countryside. As mentioned previously, Gonzalez has remained with the FARC for more than thirty years, watching her daughter join and a younger son be killed by paramilitaries in retaliation for her membership. Similarly, another woman guerrilla fighter, Lali, was interviewed by reporters. She reportedly was the one survivor of an ambush by Colombian armed forces against her unit, managing to escape with a dislocated shoulder and gunshot in the leg. She recounted a story of torturing and killing a man condemned as a war criminal by the FARC in rural southwestern Colombia.[21] These women, Lali and Eliana, come across as hardened warriors with multiple skirmishes under their belts. In many ways they are "sexless," acting as rough and aggressively as men. In contrast, Ivon Barragan Tovar seems somewhat more naïve, playing an urban spy game until finally falling victim in the midst of her first real violent operation.

Indeed, evidence suggests that women operatives join the FARC for a variety of reasons, some of which constitute coercion. Some join because they believe in the cause, of course, but others have joined because family members have been killed in skirmishes with paramilitaries and they have no place left to go or because they have been kidnapped by the FARC. For example, one reporter interviewed Soriada, who joined because seven of nine siblings in her family were members of FARC.[22] Women fighters, like the men, go through a three-week period of training before they are deployed into battle by the FARC. After they become fighters, women operatives find their lives very much controlled by FARC guidelines: relationships are permitted only between active members of FARC. This rule likely was created for operational security with the group, but as a result FARC encourages common-law marriages, rather than real marriages. Couples are not allowed to be in the same column, and children are handed over to grandparents for care.[23] After a period of time, FARC women sometimes return home to marry and have children, leaving the fight behind. While they are members of the organization, however, their lives are strictly regulated.[24]

Beyond LTTE and the FARC, Sendero Luminoso or the Shining Path in Peru also utilized female guerrilla fighters in the 1980s and early 1990s. The Shining Path was a Maoist group that operated first in the countryside of Peru and then in the cities until the early 1990s. At the height of its power, The Shining Path was estimated to have approximately 10,000 members and even managed to threaten Lima itself. According to a 1992 article published in the *New York Times*, women constituted 40 percent of its membership at that time. These women acted as recruiters in remote villages, but also participated and led guerrilla operations.[25] The Shining Path was a particularly brutal organization: between 1982 and 1992 Peruvian authorities estimated that more than 23,000 people had died from terrorist attacks perpetrated by this group.[26] Some accounts suggest that women Shining Path members were at least as brutal as their male counterparts. For example, a *Harvard Magazine* article noted in 1996 that police manuals in Peru said that Shining Path women had an "unnatural aura of witchy power about them."[27]

Perhaps the most well-known Shining Path operative was Edith Lagos. Edith Lagos was born to a wealthy businessman in Peru and went to law school before joining the Shining Path. Already a guerrilla fighter and operational leader for the Shining Path at the age of nineteen, she helped coordinate a jailbreak while still in prison.[28] In March 1982, she synchronized approximately fifty Shining Path guerrilla fighters in an attack against the Huamanga prison in Ayachuco. The attack was successful, releasing drug traffickers and Shining Path members from the prison. Edith Lagos was killed subsequently by Peruvian authorities: approximately 30,000 individuals came to her funeral.

Finally, previous chapters also discussed the role that women have played in the PKK, which operates in parts of Turkey, Iraq, and Iran.

Women PKK members played the roles of vanguard, logistician, and suicide bomber, as well as guerrilla fighters. According to some sources, the PKK established essentially a system of affirmative action for women inside the organization. This system included the High Commune of Women, which oversees among other issues women's role in the militant wing of the PKK.[29] As a result, women commanded PKK battalions and led assaults against their adversaries. Nevertheless, stories also existed on the dissatisfaction of the PKK women with their organization's leadership. In November 1998, for example, the *Kurdistan Report* published an interview with Sakine Cansiz, who at the time was the only female member of the PKK's Central Committee. She addressed these concerns directly in her commentary:

> The answer to your question as to whether or not the problem [i.e., women's inequality] has been completely overcome must be answered in the negative. There continue to be shortcomings in this area and the practical administration of ideology continues to remain an obstacle in our path. The president of the party is very concerned about resolving this question. The resolution of this problem depends on both the men and the women committing themselves to overcoming their traditional roles.[30]

The story of the PKK is particularly interesting, because it suggests that Kurdish women joined this organization in order to gain access to better opportunities than those provided in rural Kurdish society. Moreover, the leadership of the PKK viewed their organization in the same way: as helping to change Kurdish society for women as well as men. At the same time, however, the story of the PKK suggests that no matter the intentions of the PKK leadership, other fighters in this organization, male fighters, were somewhat reluctant to embrace their female counterparts. Thus, terrorist leaders had to be judicious about the integration of women into their fighting force.

In sum, Peru's Shining Path, Sri Lanka's LTTE, Nicaragua's Sandinistas, Turkey's PKK, and Colombia's FARC all utilized women extensively as guerrilla fighters in their campaigns against state authorities. Unlike in the instance of suicide bombers, the leadership of these groups articulated the role of women as revolutionary. That is, women guerrilla fighters, as leaders in their own right, were not seen as merely tools or instruments of terror, but as leaders of their groups and even movements. For the most part, most of these groups all retained a certain degree of leftist ideology. And so, this chapter confirms the traditionally held view that leftist groups were more willing to incorporate female fighters and leaders. Yet it is worth noting that none of these militant groups necessarily emerged in progressive societies or cultures. Instead, women guerrilla fighters had to struggle against cultural norms in their society even to join their respective organizations.

The next section explores the role of women as terrorists even further, focusing on women as operational leaders.

OPERATIONAL LEADERS

Operational leaders plan and execute attacks against high-profile targets, particularly attacks against civilians or in urban settings. Although it is true that men more often than not dominate in this operational arena, a few notable exceptions exist, and so it is worth further study and analysis. One exception to that general rule would be Mara Cagol, who cofounded the RB along with her husband, Renato Curcio, and Alberto Franceschini. The RB was a communist terrorist organization that operated in Italy and emerged in part out of the workers' unions in that country. Mara Cagol played an important role in shaping the direction of the RB, but Cagol also led a commando unit to free Curcio from Casale prison, playing a role as the leader of an operational cell, not just as a decision maker in the leadership council.[31] In her study of the Italian RB, Alison Jameson made the following observation:

> In general, former female members of the Red Brigades report that gender equality was maintained in the organization. But Faranda [Adriana Faranda], a member of the Rome column that carried out the 1978 kidnapping and murder of former Prime Minister Aldo Moro, recalls that at the time of her arrest in 1979, no woman had ever sat on the BR's strategy-making body, the Executive Committee. "I can't say there was any real discrimination, but I felt that the men were listened to more. Also, if any uncertainty or doubt were shown by a woman it would seem more serious."[32]

Between 1969 and 1989, 945 women were investigated for left-wing terrorist crimes in Italy, out of a total of 4,087 individuals, approximately 23.1 percent of all those investigated.[33] Interestingly, this total parallels the proportion of women guerrilla fighters in the PKK, LTTE, and FARC as well.

In his work, Daniel E. Georges-Abeyie observes that Euskadi Ta Askatasuna (ETA), the Basque separatist group in Spain, also incorporated women operational leaders in the past. For example, Genoveve Forest Tarat helped to orchestrate the 12 December 1973 assassination of Spanish Premier Admiral Carrero Blanco.[34] Indeed, most experts contend that Maria Soledad Iparraguirre Guenechea has led ETA since September 2000.[35] She represents one of two women leaders of terrorist organizations in the 21st century. The other is Comandante Ramona, the leader of the Zapatista Revolutionary Army (Ejército Zapatista de

Liberación Nacional) in Mexico.[36] Although the Zapatista Revolutionary Army is by no means religious, it does operate in culturally conservative rural Mexico, once again calling into question the assumption that women only have the opportunity to aspire to leadership roles in terrorist groups that operated in urban, leftist groups, operating primarily in Europe. However, as with these groups, women operational leaders in the Italian RB, Spanish ETA, and even Mexican Zapatistas appeared to be the exception rather than the general rule.

Nevertheless, some of the other exceptions are worth mentioning in a discussion of women operatives. Leila Khaled, of course, is one notable exception. As mentioned in Chapter 2, Leila Khaled joined the Popular Front for the Liberation of Palestine (PFLP) from her home in Lebanon's Palestinian refugee camps. In considering the myriad Palestinian resistance groups in the 1960s, Khaled's autobiography made it clear that she prioritized both the relative capabilities of the terrorist groups as well as the role that she might be able to play as a terrorist operative.[37] In August 1969, at the age of twenty-one, Leila Khaled became the first woman terrorist to hijack an airplane in the history of modern terrorism. According to news accounts, PFLP activists believed that Israeli Ambassador Rabin would be flying on the TWA flight from Rome to Tel Aviv. Leila Khaled and one other PFLP operative—calling themselves the Che Guevara unit—hijacked the plane, took the 113 passengers and seven crew hostage, and diverted the flight to Damascus.[38] All of the passengers were released with the exception of two Israelis, who were held hostage until Israel released seventy-one Arab prisoners. Although the Syrian government arrested Leila Khaled for this attack, she soon was released.

One year later, in 1970, Leila Khaled joined several colleagues to hijack four additional airplanes in a coordinated attack, including Switzerland, Germany, and the Netherlands. Khaled, along with another operative from Nicaragua, was responsible for hijacking an Israeli El Al flight from Amsterdam. She rushed the cockpit with grenades in an attempt to capture the plane, but passengers hit Khaled and her colleague over the head with bottles of whiskey, according to a report by the BBC. So this second hijacking failed and Leila Khaled was held in a British prison for twenty-eight days until the PFLP negotiated her release with the British government in exchange for other civilian hostages.[39] Despite this failure, Leila Khaled became one of the most notorious figures in the Palestinian resistance during the 1960s and 1970s.

In addition to Leila Khaled, Fusako Shigenobu was both the leader and a key operator for the Japanese Red Army (JRA), which despite the name was based in Lebanon and conducted a number of joint attacks with the PFLP against U.S., Israeli, and other Western targets in the

1970s and 1980s. Fusako Shigenobu was born in Japan and attended Meiji University. Soon thereafter she traveled to Europe where she apparently met up with Palestinian members of the PFLP. Although Fusako Shigenobu led the JRA, she also participated in some of their more notorious operations. For example, in September 1974, four JRA members assaulted the French Embassy at The Hague, taking the French ambassador hostage. In exchange for his release, the JRA asked for and received the release of a JRA operative, free passage back to Lebanon, and $300,000.[40] Fusako Shigenobu remained in Lebanon for most of her life, even after the JRA became a defunct terrorist group. Fusako Shigenobu had a child with a Palestinian man in Lebanon and kept her daughter with her in this unconventional setting as well. Shigenobu eventually was arrested in November 2000, soon after she returned to Japan from her exile in Lebanon.

Finally, the PIRA also has witnessed women in the role of operational leaders. The most infamous examples of this are Delours and Marian Price, also known as the Price sisters. Delours and Marian apparently were student teachers at Belfast University as well as PIRA operatives. They represented two of four operational leaders in a PIRA cell that conducted a series of bombings in London during the mid-1970s. Most notably, this PIRA cell placed four car bombs in downtown London on 8 March 1973. The bombs were placed outside Scotland Yard, Whitehall army recruitment center, the British Forces Broadcasting office, and Old Bailey, the Central Criminal Court. Two of these four bombs were safely defused by British authorities, but the other two killed one individual and wounded more than 200.[41] The Price sisters were arrested for this attack, tried, and imprisoned in Armagh Prison until 1980. *The Guardian* interviewed Marian in 2003, twenty years after this attack, and she still expressed no regrets:

> I have no regrets. I joined young but I knew the risks involved. I had thought long and hard. It wasn't an emotional reaction to something that happened to my family or me. It was a question of fulfilling the beliefs I still hold.[42]

Past interviews with other women operational leaders, such as Leila Khaled and Fusako Shigenobu, have exhibited strong parallels to Marian Price. For example, none of them expressed regret and still apparently hold strongly to their political ideals and grievances. One exception appears to be how they viewed the role of women in their respective revolutions. Most interviews would suggest that these women felt they had to play down their femininity and be as tough or ever rougher than their male counterparts at the time of their participation in terrorist organizations. As they have matured, however, subsequent interviews have thrown that worldview into question.[43] That is, these women still hold to their revolutionary views, but also identify other aspects of life as important. As Leila Khaled put it in 2000:

> I no longer think it's necessary to prove ourselves as women by imitating men. I have learned that a woman can be a fighter, a freedom fighter, a political activist, and that she can fall in love, and be loved, she can be married, have children, be a mother.[44]

In this sense, one can imagine that the ideals and worldview of female operational leaders, such as Leila Khaled, have paralleled the feminist movement somewhat. Strangely enough, it appears that these women have become more comfortable in taking on more male-dominated roles, even roles such as operational leaders for terrorist groups.

In sum, our research contradicts to a certain extent the prevalent assumption that terrorist groups operating in conservative cultures tend to utilize women operatives less than those operating in more progressive societies. The proportion of women operatives in the Italian RB, for example, equals the proportion of women fighters in the more culturally conservative areas of Colombia and Sri Lanka. On the other hand, this research does suggest that women fighters often have a more feminist worldview than female suicide bombers, understanding their participation in the terrorist organization both as a means of achieving political objectives and as a means of promoting women's rights in society. Indeed, it is an interesting contrast and perhaps one worth exploring further in future studies.

CONCLUSION

When people think of women as terrorists they tend to imagine suicide operatives or guerrilla fighters. It is perhaps natural to reflect on this most controversial and horrifying role that women might play in terrorist group. Of course, women play other roles as well, clarified to a certain degree in this book. Societies, however, appear to struggle more with the concept of female terrorist operatives than political vanguards, logisticians, or recruiters. Nevertheless, the motivations of female operatives do not appear to differ much from their male counterparts. Perhaps female operatives personalize the political struggle much more than men, viewing it in terms of a feminist movement as well as a political movement. Leila Khaled's autobiography would certainly suggest that this is the case, although some of the evidence from the Chechen female suicide bombers would suggest otherwise. Clearly, women fighters experience the political struggle differently: recall the PKK's struggle with sexual harassment among the ranks of its fighters.

In the end, the story of women as operatives underscores the complexity of terrorism studies in general. Individual terrorists might articulate different objectives. Internal group dynamics often confound or even have a greater influence on terrorist leaders' decision making, and terrorist groups, both foot soldiers and leaders, interact with and respond to community pressure in myriad ways. Countering terrorist group dynamics and motivations, therefore, is not an easy task. This book by no means is meant to imply that counterterrorism officials handle the issue of female terrorists any differently than that of male terrorists. Rather, it is meant to reinforce our belief that we still have much to learn. Moreover, terrorism's complexity, however difficult, in the end is often a reflection of the wider challenges faced by leaders and citizens worldwide.

6

Women as Political Vanguards

A number of the stories in previous chapters tell of women terrorists whose exploits took on almost legendary proportions in their communities as well as the media. Leila Khaled, for example, became a sex symbol in her pursuit of Palestinian independence as an operational leader for the Popular Front for the Liberation of Palestine (PFLP). Black Fatima grew to be Russia's equivalent of the Wicked Witch of the West for the Chechen insurgency and the recruitment of female suicide bombers in those communities. Similarly, Peruvian supporters of Sendero Luminoso, or the Shining Path, heralded Edith Lagos arguably far more than her guerrilla skirmishes deserved. In this sense, the notoriety of these women terrorists was derived from their gender more often than not, rather than their strategic thinking, creativity, or even operational prowess.

For the most part, these women served as logisticians, recruiters, suicide bombers, and guerrilla fighters for their terrorist and insurgent group, and throughout previous chapters, we have revealed that women often play significant—if understudied—roles in sustaining the forward progression or even survival of terrorist and insurgent organizations. Yet it is rare for women to assume leadership positions in these groups that they risked so much for over the years. Cultural and organizational barriers have prevented the promotion of women as terrorists, just as in nonviolent organizations and roles.

Every now and then, however, women have served as political vanguards for their respective terrorist and insurgent groups. According to the Merriam-Webster Online Dictionary, a vanguard is always at the "forefront of an action or a movement."[1] Often this vanguard personifies the intent and commitment of a particular terrorist or insurgent group. When examining the history of most terrorist and insurgent organizations, "vanguard" is not a term that would apply to many women involved in these groups. The ideological and strategic leaders of terrorist groups have traditionally been men, inasmuch as the groups themselves and the use of violence is a domain largely inhabited by men. Indeed, the more well-known vanguards throughout history—Che Guevara in Guatemala, Mao Tse-tung in China, Gerry Adams in Northern Ireland, Hassan Nasrallah in Lebanon, Yasser Arafat in the Palestinian territories, and of course, Osama Bin Laden and Ayman al-Zawahiri—are all men. Although most of these individuals are household names, there are few women in a similar position who could be considered well known for their leadership and strategic vision.

In fact, most students of political violence and militancy often are surprised to learn that throughout history there have been some very influential women who, although limited by gender roles, have impacted their specific movements in significant ways. For example, most students of terrorism are familiar with Abimael Guzmán, the founder and leader of the Shining Path in Peru, which was responsible for the deaths of thousands of civilians in the 1980s and 1990s in that country. Yet it is less well known that his wife and companion—Augusta LaTorre and Elena Iparraguirre, respectively—also had significant influence over the ideology and direction of the Shining Path. Like Abimael Guzmán, Augusta LaTorre lived in Ayacucho, Peru. She was the daughter of a local banker, and her father also was the head of the Communist party in Huanta. Through her father, Augusta LaTorre met Abimael Guzmán. According to a well-known journalist who lived in and reported on Peru, Robin Kirk, Augusta was a mediocre student but fell in love with Guzmán and so read everything on Communist ideology that he suggested. Augusta also pushed Guzmán to become more and more extreme in his ideology and activities.[2]

After their marriage, Guzmán appointed Augusta LaTorre the head of the Popular Woman's Movement, and she traveled with him to China to study about Mao Zedong and the Long March. Upon their return, Augusta LaTorre and Abimael Guzmán encountered Peruvian security forces during a protest, and she was beaten badly. The couple subsequently went underground, and stories about Augusta LaTorre's violence and commitment to the Shining Path spread widely. Referred to as Comrade Norah, she apparently tried to execute her aunt and uncle in 1982 for refusing to sell weapons to the Shining Path.[3]

Augusta LaTorre died in 1988 of unknown causes. Some speculated at the time that she committed suicide or she was killed with the approval of Abimael Guzmán himself for threatening to leave him and the Shining Path. Nonetheless, her funeral was taped by the Shining Path, and she was held up as an ideal operative for future generations. Similarly, known as Comrade Miriam, Elena Iparraguirre succeeded

Augusta LaTorre as Abimael Guzmán's lover and companion. She was a school teacher who joined the Shining Path in 1982 and quickly rose to prominence in its leadership council. Elena Iparraguirre was arrested along with Guzmán in 1992 by Peruvian security authorities. She was sentenced to a lifetime in prison for her role in the Shining Path, but apparently continued to live with Abimael Guzmán in prison until 2005.[4]

Other examples exist of women as political vanguards in terrorist and insurgent groups. These women have led their organizations and provided strategic guidance and yet are less well known in the annals of terrorism history. They include Kesire Yildirim from the Partiya Karkerên Kurdistan (PKK), or the Kurdish Workers' Party, in Turkey; Bernadette Sands-McKevitt from the Real Irish Republican Army (RIRA) in Northern Ireland; Comandante Ramona from the Zapatista Revolutionary Army (or Ejército Zapatista de Liberación Nacional) in Mexico; Maria Soledad Iparraguirre Guenechea from the Basque Fatherland and Freedom group (Euskadi Ta Askatasuna, or ETA) in Spain; Rima Fakhry from Hizballah in Lebanon; and even Fusako Shigenobu from the Japanese Red Army (JRA). Indeed, in our analysis of twenty-two different terrorist and insurgent groups, we discovered that twelve utilized women as political vanguards. This chapter examines women who have risen to prominence in their respective terrorist and insurgent organizations and who have had an enduring impact on their respective militant group's direction, successes, and failures.

To do this, we discuss three different categories of women as political vanguards. First, "strategic visionaries" are women who have revolutionized the ideology or strategy of a terrorist or insurgent group. For the most part, women as strategic visionaries are journalists, authors, or philosophers who have written manifestos and pamphlets that provide strategic guidance to terrorist leaders. Women as strategic visionaries sometimes are involved in militant activities themselves, but not always. They also differ somewhat from propagandists, because their role is less to garner new recruits as to provide a strategic worldview and direction.

Second, "central committee members" are women who have participated in decision-making bodies for terrorist and insurgent groups. These women might or might not be strategic visionaries, but, like Elena Iparraguirre from the Shining Path in Peru, they essentially comprise the cabinet secretaries or even the supreme leaders of terrorist groups. That is, these women act on the strategic visions provided in the aforementioned categories. Their decisions may relate to military operations, but also charitable activities and women's rights within the communities. Sometimes these women achieve a position in their respective terrorist and insurgent group's central committee based on past contributions to the group itself, while at other times it appears that family ties helped them achieve these positions.

Finally, "political officials" are women who have been elected to serve in civilian legislatures to some degree, but yet still are well-known members of terrorist and insurgent groups. These women might not have served in leadership positions within the terrorist or insurgent group itself. Sometimes, they are the wives, mothers, or sisters of well-known terrorist leaders or activists and so win political notoriety based on these relationships. Nonetheless, because they are elected officials, they sometimes are seen as voicing the needs of the terrorist group itself or their supporters.

STRATEGIC VISIONARIES

Strategic visionaries are individuals within the terrorist group or wider movement who publish manifestos, pamphlets, and other documents that outline its worldview and direction. These individuals sometimes are propagandists, but they also can be senior leaders within the terrorist and insurgent group itself. Naim Qassam, for example, published a book titled *Hizballah: The Story from Within* in 2005. At that time, Naim Qassam was the deputy secretary for Lebanese Hizballah. Hizballah fought to remove Israeli security forces from Lebanon from 1983 until 2000. In May 2000, Israel withdrew its forces from southern Lebanon, but retained control over a small parcel of land often referred to as Shebaa Farms. Hizballah used this presence to continue its fight against Israel, albeit on a smaller scale until the summer of 2006, at which point hostilities erupted again. Naim Qassam often has been considered the strategic visionary for Hizballah in partnership with its leader, Hassan Nasrallah.

Following Israeli withdrawal from southern Lebanon in May 2000, for example, many within Lebanon questioned the purpose of Hizballah's existence, and Naim Qassam was tasked with answering these questions. In *Hizballah: The Story from Within*, Qassam explained the rationale behind Hizballah's transformation and shift toward becoming a Lebanese political party and reaching out to other states beyond Iran to form strategic relationships:

> [Hizballah's] commitment to the Jurist–Theologian [Khameini] and his jurisprudence does not limit the scope of internal work at the level of forging relations with the various powers and constituents of Lebanon. It further does not limit the sphere of regional and international cooperation with groups with whom the Party's strategic direction or concerns meet.[5]

By writing *Hizballah: The Story from Within* and taking on the role of deputy secretary for Hizballah, it is arguable that Naim Qassam fulfilled the role of strategic visionary. Somewhat different than a propagandist, these activities justified and outlined the strategic rationale behind shifts in Hizballah's behavior and direction.

Of course, not all terrorist and insurgent groups necessarily have strategic visionaries in their midst. The Revolutionary Armed Forces of Colombia (FARC), for example, could arguably be considered as lacking a strategic visionary. Although the FARC has its roots in the Marxist–Leninist movement, it had become deeply involved in the drug economy by the 1990s. Moreover, despite its ideological roots, FARC leaders did not outline or explain the rationale for this shift and how it contributed to its overall agenda. Of course, it is well known that FARC leaders meet periodically to conduct what one might call operational planning or setting short-term objectives. Yet it is difficult to identify an individual who could be called "strategic visionary" within the organization.

With regards to women as strategic visionaries, our analysis identified several women who could be considered as having contributed significantly to the strategic direction or ideology of their terrorist and insurgent group. Ironically, most of these women founded or were at the helm of largely secular leftist terrorist organizations that had their roots in the 1960s and 1970s. Very few contemporary women can be credibly identified as driving the ideology or strategic vision of their respective groups. There are several reasons posited for this trend. The first is that many of the women involved in leftist groups in the 1970s were products of the feminist movement that was sweeping the Western world. Alternatively, some posit that fewer women appear in leadership positions in the 21st century because terrorism in this decade has been dominated by religiously conservative groups, such as al-Qa'ida, the Taliban, and others that have not permitted nor desired women to take a more prominent role. As a result, more women in these groups are trying to demonstrate their commitment and find their "voice," so to speak, through operational prowess. For the purposes of our discussion on women as strategists, we focus on four women who for a variety of reasons were able to play prominent roles in their organizations as strategic thinkers and visionaries.

For example, Gudrun Ensslin was one of the top leaders of the German Baader-Meinhof Gang, also known as the Red Army Faction (RAF). Gudrun Ensslin cofounded the Baader-Meinhof Gang, along with Ulrike Meinhof, a prominent German left-wing journalist, and Andreas Baader, an intelligent, rebellious youth with a criminal past. At its creation, the Baader-Meinhof Gang was comprised largely of middle-class youths, and it primarily targeted German elites, because they represented the establishment, and were a reincarnation of the Third Reich.[6] In addition, the Baader-Meinhof Gang often attacked police stations and policemen, robbed banks to buy weapons and was responsible for an attack on a U.S. military base in Germany.[7]

Among Baader-Meinhoff's three leaders, Gudrun Ensslin reportedly was responsible for the group's finances and even dictated training to a certain extent: for example, Ensslin had the final say on whether or not Baader-Meinhof members would train in the Middle East.[8] According to Eileen MacDonald, author of *Shoot the Women First*, beyond the day-to-day management of Baader-Meinhof, Ensslin also was "the soul of Baader-Meinhof," with Meinhof as its "head," and Baader as its "engine."[9] That is, Ensslin made significant contributions to Baader-Meinhof's leftist ideals and strategic direction.

Active in left-wing student politics and well-known for her radical leftist views, Ensslin first put her Marxist theory into practice in 1968 with Baader, her boyfriend, by bombing two department stores in Frankfurt. Notably, a significant portion of the German population sympathized at that time with the Baader-Meinhof group's leftist ideals, if not their violent tactics. Alternatively, others saw the group as lacking political goals and only engaged in nihilism. Importantly, Ulrike Meinhof also played the role of strategic visionary for the Baader-Meinhof Gang, along with Ensslin. In fact, Meinhof penned the RAF's manifesto, *The Concept of the Urban Guerilla*, in 1968. Nevertheless, many experts believe that Ensslin made significant contributions to this book and, indeed, attributed many of the ideas contained in this book as originating from Ensslin rather than Meinhof. According to Eileen MacDonald's interview with Bommi Baumann, the leader of another German revolutionary group, for example, Ensslin was "… an extremely intelligent woman; very into it, fanatical, and she could talk." By contrast, Baumann testified that Baader was "… aggressive, rude, and not very intellectual."[10] These observations suggest that Ensslin played the role of strategic visionary in the Baader-Meinhof Gang, perhaps more than but at the very least along with Ulrike Meinhof.

Susanna Ronconi represents another strategic visionary in the world of terrorism and insurgency. Like Ensslin and Meinhof in the Baader-Meinhof Gang, Susanna Ronconi was the cofounder of the now-defunct Italian terrorist group Prima Linea (or Front Line). Ronconi initially joined the most notorious Italian militant organization, the Red Brigades (RB), in 1974 because she had been actively involved in feminist causes and believed that the RB would offer her an opportunity to continue to further those causes. Moreover, Ronconi also believed that joining the RB would give her the sense of family and belonging that she desired.[11] She was incorrect on both accounts. Despite the fact that the group was cofounded by a woman, Mara Cagol, the RB turned out not to be particularly concerned about feminism, although former members report that in general, the group maintained gender equality.[12] Moreover, prior to joining the RB, Ronconi had been actively involved in feminist and other leftist causes above ground. The stark shift to an underground lifestyle where the militants were forced to sever all contacts with their families and society, where rules had to be strictly followed, and where there were few women led Ronconi to describe her time in the Brigades as lonely.[13]

During her time with the RB, Ronconi was responsible for the death of five individuals.[14] For example, she was involved in the planning of the murder of several individuals, including two judges, who were working to foil Red Brigades attacks. She had also been involved in bank robberies, kneecappings, attempted assassinations, and theft.[15] Ronconi decided to leave the RB after her boyfriend, who was also a member of the Brigades, was arrested while they were on the run.[16] She fled to Turin and cofounded Prima Linea as a four-person, all-woman offshoot of the RB. The group, opposed by the men of the RB,[17] was solely dedicated to carrying out violent actions relevant to the feminist cause, to "advance the protagonism of women through the armed struggle," and was dedicated to serving the needs of the working class. They saw themselves as protectors of women and the working class and took violent action against those exploiting either group.

Prima Linea did not intend to seek political power like the RB. Instead, the group's motto was "Prima Linea is founded to prepare its own destruction."[18] Ronconi and her cofounders structured the group very differently from the RB to maximize social interaction between the group's members and also their community of supporters.[19] Ronconi, who had no children and as an underground terrorist operative had no family other than the one she created through her association with the group, reportedly threw all of her energy into Prima Linea. Interestingly, through Prima Linea, Ronconi advanced the idea that a woman's maternal sense actually makes her a natural purveyor of violence: at the time of a child's birth, it is only the mother who has the power to either give life or take it away.[20] Ronconi became so dedicated to the group that when it became clear that she had to choose between her lover, who wanted to leave the group, and staying loyal to the organization, she chose to remain with Prima Linea.[21] According to an interview provided by Ronconi to Eileen MacDonald, her memories of her years in Prima Linea "... riddled with bullets and death, were also happy memories for her because she had felt so at home with others who were as committed as she was to the armed struggle."[22]

Prima Linea initially focused on small-scale attacks against Italian fascists, but quickly moved on to shootings, arson, armed robbery, kidnapping, and murder.[23] One of the more well-known Prima Linea attacks was the shooting of a female prison guard for mistreating the women prisoners.[24] Like Gudrun Ensslin of the Baader-Meinhof group, Ronconi was directly involved in planning and executing many Prima Linea attacks, including one in which she led a group of Prima Linea militants to conduct a raid on the Turin School of Industrial Management, took 190 students and professors hostages, and kneecapped ten of them. Ronconi was later arrested and imprisoned for her activities, but remained committed to some of the same feminist ideals and defended her decision to engage in violence to achieve political ends.

Additionally, Fusako Shigenobu, known as the Red Queen, established the now-defunct JRA in 1971, a Marxist–Leninist terrorist group that aimed to overthrow the Japanese government and monarchy through violence and usher in a world united under communism. The JRA, a small group of thirty to forty at its zenith, trained in Palestinian refugee camps in Lebanon, facilitated by Shigenobu's contacts with the Marxist PFLP. Shigenobu, who radicalized in the Marxist–Leninist ideology by participating in Tokyo University sit-ins,[25] believed and convinced the other JRA members that the Palestinians would lead the leftist revolution and that it would spread to Japan.[26]

The JRA carried out bombings, primarily of foreign embassies, and airplane hijackings.[27] Some of its major attacks, many of which were masterminded by Shigenobu, include a machine gun and grenade attack in 1972 at Lod Airport in Israel resulting in twenty-six deaths and eighty injuries; two Japanese airline hijackings in 1973 and 1977; hostage-taking at several embassies, including the U.S. embassy in Kuala Lumpur, Malaysia; and a 1988 bombing of a U.S. military recreational club in Naples, Italy, which killed five Americans.[28]

Much like the previous two strategic visionaries, Shigenobu's status as the leader of a revolutionary movement came with personal cost. Although her daughter lived with her in Lebanon, she had to disappear to plan and execute attacks for months at a time, leaving her daughter's care in the hands of fellow revolutionaries. From prison, Shigenobu wrote a book about her relationship with her daughter and expressed regret that she did not have a normal childhood.[29] Although Shigenbou was at the helm of a group that engaged in murder and spread mayhem around the world for over a decade, her daughter, who spent her early years with her mother in a Palestinian refugee camp in Lebanon, says that Shigenobu, who was arrested in 2000 after sneaking back into Japan from Lebanon on a false passport, was a good mother and a sweet person and has received bad press for her past activities.[30]

In 2001, from her prison cell, Shigenobu announced the dissolution of the JRA. In February 2006, Shigenobu was sentenced by a Japanese court to twenty years in prison for a JRA attack on the French embassy in The Hague in 1974 in which the ambassador and several others were taken hostage. The court acknowledged that Shigenobu was "... a leader and the central figure of the group."[31] Shigenobu expressed regret over the deaths that resulted from the 1972 attack on Lod Airport but defended the attack itself.[32] She also lamented the "death" of the group's ideals, while at the same time still vowing to continue the struggle, despite the fact that the movement had ended. She said "The verdict is not the end. It is only the beginning. Strong will shall keep spreading."[33]

Finally, Kesire Yildirim was a founding member of the PKK in Turkey and wife of its leader, Abdullah Ocalan. Kesire Yildirim apparently met Abdullah Ocalan while in college and became a believer in both its articulated Marxist–Leninist ideology and the Kurdish nationalist movement. As the first and only female member of the PKK's central committee in 1978, Kesire Yildirim is credited by most, including Abdullah Ocalan, for embedding feminist ideals into the PKK's strategic worldview and direction. Under her guidance, the PKK became an organization that fought to provide better opportunities for Kurdish rural women in Turkey.[34] Interestingly, Kesire Yildirim divorced Abdullah Ocalan in 1987 and left the PKK. According to most sources, this split was the result of differences in the strategic directly for the PKK. Indeed, Yildirim established a splinter organization, called the PKK–Veijin, soon thereafter. Around this time in PKK history, it was well known that Ocalan was attempting to kill most of his opponents within the wider Kurdish movement. So it is interesting that Yildirim survived. In a subsequent interview, Ocalan actually commented that other members of the PKK's central committee wanted to assassinate Yildirim for treason, but he persuaded them to decide otherwise.[35] Truth or fiction, Kesire Yildirim eventually took sanctuary in Sweden.

In sum, our analysis of twenty-two different terrorist and insurgent groups only revealed four groups with women as strategic visionaries. These women provided strategic guidance and direction to their respective militant groups, either through personal relationships with their leadership, as a leader themselves, or through written manifestos and pamphlets. Interestingly, most of these women were part of relatively secular movements. Moreover, their activities as strategic visionaries also reflected their desire for women's equality in general.

The following section explores the role of women in central leadership committees. We discovered, through our research, that women tend to take on this role more than that of strategic visionary. Yet strong similarities exist between the two roles, both representing forms of women as political vanguards.

CENTRAL COMMITTEE MEMBERS

Although some examples exist of women as strategic visionaries, this role is less evident in terrorist and insurgent groups. Nonetheless, women have taken on leadership positions in the central committees of terrorist and insurgent groups throughout history. Sometimes these women are in charge of social and charitable activities, or perhaps even women's issues. Regardless, by obtaining a position in the central committee, women have influence over the strategic direction of a terrorist or insurgent group and therefore can be considered "vanguards."

Most militant groups have some form of central leadership committee. Documents obtained by U.S. forces in Afghanistan during Operation Enduring Freedom, for example, revealed letters written in the 1990s by al-Qa'ida operatives to senior leadership residing in Sudan. These letters asked for strategic guidance and resources, indicating some form of bureaucracy and central committee within the al-Qa'ida structure at that time.[36] Similarly, Lebanese Hizballah, Palestinian Hamas (Harakat al-Muqawama al-Islamiyya), the Kurdish Workers' Party in Turkey, the Provisional Irish Republican Army in Northern Ireland, the Basque Fatherland and Freedom group in Spain, the Shining Path in Peru, and Baader-Meinhof Gang all are known to have had a central committee over the years. And while women have not functioned as members of the central leadership committees for all of these groups, they have taken on this role in some of them.

For example, as mentioned previously, both Augusta LaTorre and Elena Iparraguirre were members of the Shining Path's central committee, along with other women, during the 1980s and 1990s. Kesire Yildirim also was a founding member of the PKK in Turkey in the 1970s and a member of its central committee. Subsequently, in the late 1990s, Sakine Cansiz also was the sole female member of the PKK's central committee. So these women as central committee members present an interesting contrast to the seeming lack of women as strategic visionaries in terrorist and insurgent groups.

Another woman who was a member of a central committee for an insurgent group during the 1990s was "Comandante Ramona." Comandante Ramona was a member of the Clandestine Revolutionary Indigenous Committee, or the central leadership committee of the Zapatistas in Mexico.[37] The Zapatistas were a popular peasant movement that represented indigenous peoples in Mexico. Comandante Ramona by all accounts was the deputy commander of this group. Indeed, she helped take control of the Mexican city San Cristobal during the 1994 Zapatista uprising. A Tzotzil Indian, Comandante Ramona advocated publicly not only for the rights of peasant farmers but also for women's equality in Mexico's indigenous populations. For example, in 1997, Comandante Ramona issued the following statement:

> You know the farmers (campesinos) situation, the injustice and the poverty in which the indigenous women live in our country. Every day that the supreme government continues with politics in favor of the rich, this situation becomes more difficult. We, the women, are victims of the lack of education, of not having jobs, of daily violence, of health situations ever so much worse … That is why we struggle for the autonomy of the Indian pueblos … to take in our hands the control of our lives and not suffer so much.[38]

Comandante Ramona died in January 2006 of kidney disease at the age of 47. She was heralded by the current head of the Zapatistas as one of the key and tireless leaders of the Zapatista movement over the years.

In addition to Comandante Ramona and the other women members of central committees, listed above, the case of Bernadette Sands-McKevitt is also worth exploring further. Bernadette Sands-McKevitt was a member and supporter of the Provisional Irish Republican Army (PIRA) in Northern Ireland. Her brother, Bobby Sands, died during a hunger strike in the 1980s while in prison and, in many ways, symbolized the heart and commitment of the Republican movement at that time and in subsequent years. Similarly, Bernadette Sands-McKevitt's husband, Michael McKevitt, was the Quartermaster General of the PIRA in the 1990s.[39] So, for the most part, Sands-McKevitt's relationship to the PIRA came through family members, rather than based on her own activities. That relationship changed, however, during the Good Friday Accords in the late 1990s. Sands-McKevitt, her parents, and siblings all opposed the Good Friday Accords publicly. In a 1997 interview, moreover, Sands-McKevitt announced the creation of an opposition group,

> I know there is a lot of confusion and a lot of people are wondering what exactly is the 32 County Sovereignty Committee about. 32 County Sovereignty Committee has come about over the last 3 weeks. It has formed as a pressure group. But for some time now a lot of people, a lot of concerned people in Ireland have been watching the situation unfolding [author's note: Good Friday Accords] and have … as events have unfolded have become more and more concerned at the direction things are going. …[40]

The 32 County Sovereignty Committee was a political front organization, headed by Bernadette Sands-McKevitt. Indeed, along with her husband, Bernadette Sands-McKevitt even went so far as to establish the Real IRA, a splinter off of the PIRA. The Real IRA opposed the peace process in Northern Ireland and became active in the period between 1998 and 2001, for example, placing a car bomb outside the BBC headquarters in London.

She and her husband were eventually arrested by British security forces in 2001.

Maria Soledad Iparraguirre Guenechea represents yet another woman who was a member of a central leadership committee in a terrorist or insurgent group. Soledad Iparraguirre's family ran safe houses for the Basque Fatherland and Freedom movement when she was a child. So it is perhaps not surprising that she began to work with the Vizcaya commando unit while a teenager in the late 1970s, primarily as a courier. According to Spanish authorities, Soledad Iparraguirre then moved to work for the Araba commando in the mid-1980s and conducted her first attack on a police patrol in March 1985.[41] Eventually known by the alias "Anboto," Soledad Iparraguirre expanded her capabilities and authority within ETA during the 1990s. For example, Spanish authorities believe that she was partly responsible for an assassination attempt on King Juan Carlos in 1997. Indeed, Soledad Iparraguirre became the only female member of ETA's central committee in 2000 at the age of 39. At that time, she was essentially in charge of military operations, while her romantic partner was the head of ETA's political wing. Four years later, in 2004, Soledad Iparraguirre, her partner, and her son were arrested by Spanish authorities.

Finally, Rima Fakhry is the only female member of Hizballah's political bureau. First nominated for this position in 2005 at the age of 39 years old, Rima Fakhry did not come from a Hizballah family, nor was her husband a member of Hizballah. Indeed, she attended the American University in Beirut as a youth and received a degree in agricultural science.[42] After Rima Fakhry graduated from the American University, she became involved with Hizballah youth organizations and eventually came to oversee the women's organizations in Beirut. A mother of four children, Rima Fakhry has discussed the role of women in Hizballah for the media, stating, "Women play an equal role to men and they perform the same tasks except for those directly related to armed resistance.... They participate in all fields—education, health, media, literacy campaigns, et cetera."[43] Nonetheless, Hizballah clearly struggled over the appropriate role for women in this organization. In previous chapters, we discussed how Hizballah women have taken on the roles of logistician, which has been the primary focus of their activities in the past.[44] Beginning in 2004, however, Hizballah leaders reportedly determined in a conference to approve a recommendation to allow women into the political bureau as well as other political institutions. Rima Fakhry, as head of the women's organizations in Beirut, represented a natural first choice. Hizballah also decided to allow women to run in municipal elections as part of their party. Yet Hizballah did not include women candidates on its national ticket at that time. So this suggests that while women have begun to make an impact on the strategic direction of Hizballah, their degree of influence in the role of political vanguards is still somewhat questionable.

In sum, a number of women have played the role of political vanguards through their participation in central leadership committees for terrorist and insurgent groups. In these committees, sometimes women have taken charge of military operations, as did Soledad Iparraguirre for ETA in Spain and Comandante Ramona in Mexico. At other times, these women have been placed in charge of overseeing women's equality, not only within the terrorist and insurgent group itself but in the wider population of supporters for a particular group. This appears to be the case for Sakine Cansiz, a central committee member for the PKK in Turkey. In all three cases, these women rose through the ranks of their respective groups and movements to take on these leadership roles.

Interestingly, our analysis also revealed several women who have assumed roles in the leadership of terrorist or insurgent groups simply through marriage or other family ties. This observation could be made for Elena Iparraguirre, for example, in the Shining Path, as well as Bernadette Sands-McKevitt in the Real Irish Republican Army. That is, we are not arguing that these women did not play a significant role in the central committees once they had a place at the table, but rather that place likely would not have been granted to them without these familial ties.

The next section explores women who have become political officials and in many ways representatives for their terrorist and insurgent groups in local and national governments.

POLITICAL OFFICIALS

Sometimes terrorist and insurgent groups achieve legitimacy through negotiations with a central government or even military success. In these instances, it is not unusual for members of the terrorist or insurgent group to assume political positions within the central government itself. For example, Yasser Arafat was the leader of Fatah and chairman of the Palestine Liberation Organization in the 1970s and 1980s. After the Oslo Accords and the initiation of the Palestinian-Israeli peace process, however, Arafat was elected president of the Palestinian Authority and retained this position from 1995 until 2004. Similarly, Hussein Amin was a senior leader for the Moro Nationalist Liberation Front (MNLF) in the 1990s, which fought to wrestle autonomous control over Mindanao away from the central government of the Philippines. After the 1996 Davao Peace Accords, Hussein Amin ran for national office and became the Congressional Representative for Sulu's 1st District. Of course, both of these examples constitute male terrorist leaders who subsequently became elected officials in their respective countries following a negotiated peace deal. But some examples of women also exist. As was mentioned in previous chapters, Dora Maria Telles Arguello, for example, fought for the Sandinista National Liberation Front against a dictatorial regime in Nicaragua during the 1970s. After the Sandinistas gained control of that country, Dora Maria Telles Arguello became the Minister of Health. Telles, in this sense, represented a political vanguard for her militant group, as she rose to leadership not only within the group itself, but also in the wider Nicaraguan community.

Given the male-dominated nature of terrorist and insurgent groups, students might be surprised to find women elected or nominated as political officials to represent these group in the central government. Yet our research and analysis revealed multiple examples of women serving as political officials in this way. Perhaps some of the most interesting examples are the women of Hamas. Hamas is a Palestinian terrorist group that articulates both Islamist and nationalist objectives. On 11 November 2004 Palestinian President Arafat passed away, and Fatah moved quickly to nominate his replacement, Mahmud Abbas. This change in Palestinian Authority leadership provided Hamas with the opportunity to challenge Fatah for leadership of the Palestinian national movement. Indeed, between December 2004 and May 2005 a series of elections was held in the West Bank and Gaza Strip, including the presidential elections as well as municipal elections. The municipal elections represented the first in approximately 20 years. Subsequently, in January 2007, elections were held for the Palestinian Legislative Council, approximately ten years after the first series of elections for that governing body. Thus, the thirteen months between December 2005 and January 2007 represented a time for Palestinians to revisit their trust in the political factions as well as their understanding of the Palestinian resistance and voice these views through their votes.

In previous years, Hamas leaders had voiced a willingness to participate in local elections, such as student and municipal elections, but not Palestinian national elections. According to most experts, this reluctance was based on an unwillingness to legitimize or approve the Oslo Accords. Indeed, Hamas' unwillingness to participate in national elections caused a split in Hamas in the mid-1990s and the emergence of a new political party, Khalas. Hamas leaders changed their position on national elections during the al-Aqsa Intifada and ran candidates in both municipal and national elections. These candidates were nominated for political office under the "Change and Reform Party," sponsored by Hamas.

Beginning in July 2005, political parties began to identify candidates for the Palestinian Legislative Council. According to most accounts, Hamas chose its candidates based on credibility and support in their resident district. Fatah, in contrast, for the most part favored stalwart party members. As late as 6 January 2006, opinion polls suggested that a pattern would emerge in the legislative elections similar to what happened in the municipal elections. That is, Hamas would make a strong showing, but Fatah candidates would still win a majority of seats. For example, a poll conducted by An Najah National University in Nablus, a noted Hamas stronghold, found that 39.3 percent of respondents planned to vote for Fatah, while 31.3 percent expected to vote for Hamas.[45] The expectation inside Israel and the Palestinian Authority that Fatah would continue to dominate Palestinian politics was therefore reasonable.

But voters surprised the political commentators and pollsters later that month. For the Palestinian Legislative Council, representatives were elected proportionately, based on total votes cast for candidate lists nationally, as well as geographically, based on total votes cast for specific individuals by district. For the most part, well-known Hamas figures ran on the proportional lists, while respected local leaders ran on the geographic lists. Hamas candidates from both candidate lists fared well and, thus, it won an outright majority in the elections. Specifically, Hamas won twenty-nine of sixty-six seats from the proportional lists. Five of Hamas' twenty-nine seats from the proportional lists went to women candidates. Hamas also won forty-four of sixty-six seats from the geographic lists, and four independent candidates sponsored by Hamas also won seats in the geographic election, bringing their total to 77 out of 132 total seats.

What is particularly interesting about the five women candidates and Hamas' electoral victory is that they were placed on the proportional lists. That is, Palestinians voted in these women by voting for the "Change and Reform Party," not the women themselves. In this way, Hamas leaders arguably gave the women candidates a *better chance* at becoming elected officials, primarily because their possible election was tied directly to the election of famous Hamas figures.

In addition to the "Change and Reform" party in the Palestinian territories, Sinn Fein is another political party often viewed as a front organization for a terrorist or insurgent group. Sinn Fein, in this sense, has been associated most closely with the Provisional Irish Republican Army in Northern Ireland. As discussed in previous chapters, women have played significant roles as logisticians, recruiters, and operational leaders for the PIRA. While women have not risen to strategic leadership positions within the PIRA itself, moreover, they have been candidates for political office.

For example, Northern Ireland held elections for its Assembly in March 2007. Under the Good Friday Accords, this Assembly essentially functions as the Parliament or the Congress for Northern Ireland in semi-autonomous rule. Sinn Fein members ran on a platform that supported the peace process, advocated an end to British direct rule, and would deliver social and economic programs to Republican neighborhoods. It also included a section on equality for women and elderly people in its manifesto. The following statement was taken from the introduction of the Sinn Fein platform,

> The peace process has transformed Irish society. Problems that only a decade ago seemed intractable are now being addressed one by one. In the post-Good Friday Agreement period, increased all-Ireland cooperation is creating huge opportunities for everyone. Sinn Féin has driven the peace process. As the only all-Ireland party, we continue to drive the agenda for positive change.[46]

This manifesto was particularly interesting because it featured women candidates prominently on the cover as well as throughout the document. Indeed, in the March 2007 Assembly Elections for Northern Ireland, 28 Sinn Fein candidates won seats in the Assembly, out of a possible 108. The only party to win greater representation was the Democratic Unionist Party, which obtained 36 seats. Significantly, of Sinn Fein's 28 total seats, eight went to women candidates.

In sum, some terrorist and insurgent groups over the years have established political parties or front organizations in order to provide a nonviolent face to their support communities and the world. These front organizations provide opportunities for women to become involved with the terrorist group and even take on leadership positions, without being involved directly in militant activities. Two different terrorist organizations, in this context, have utilized women as political officials: Hamas and the PIRA. Due to the public nature of their activities, these women often garnered significant attention and so were seen as political leaders of their respective organizations, at least to a certain degree.

CONCLUSION

Despite the fact that women have sought equality with men in terrorist and insurgent groups since the 1960s, few actually have been able to achieve leadership roles within these organizations. More often than not, terrorist and insurgent leaders exploit women for strategic or tactical purposes in a way that serves the needs of the militant group, but undermines secondary considerations such as the liberation of women or women's equality.

Interestingly, women who are able to gain a position within terrorist or insurgent groups often articulate feelings of liberation and pride in having won this "right." Yet it is debatable whether or not this translates into actual leadership roles or decision-making power.

Indeed, the examples in this chapter suggest that several patterns exist in women as political vanguards. In a select few instances, women have been able to act as strategic visionaries, especially if they were involved in the founding of a particular terrorist or insurgent group. Women as political vanguards more regularly appear to have become members of a terrorist or insurgent group's central committee. But, even in these examples, only a limited number achieved this position on their own merit versus through family ties or even marriage. Moreover, we find it difficult to cite women's ability to gain the "right" to kill civilians as part of a terrorist activity or even the right to provide strategic guidance to a terrorist campaign as progress. This progress, in our minds, is outweighed by the havoc wreaked by escalatory back-and-forth attacks that often occur between terrorist and counterterrorist forces, by the economic impoverishment and curfews that often accompany escalating violence, and the constant fear experienced by women on both sides of these struggles.

Finally, in an alternative pattern, women as vanguards have been put forth as political candidates and officials in the rare circumstances that militant groups have been able to gain standing within the central government. Only this last pattern provides any evidence that women's liberation and progress can be gained through participation in a fringe movement of this nature. In this sense, the experiences of Nicaragua, Northern Ireland, and the Palestinian territories can be instructive. The question then becomes whether these small victories represent pinpricks of light in the midst of horrendous chaos and suffering or whether they are anomalies in and of themselves. It is a disturbing thought.

Women as Terrorists: Past, Present, and Future

Since the advent of modern terrorism in 1968, women have played a small but expanding role in terrorist organizations and their corresponding revolutionary movements. While men continue to dominate the leadership of terrorist groups around the world, women have taken on the responsibility of providing logistical support, recruiting new members, and even creating a veil of protection around their male counterparts in clandestine organizations. In some instances, women terrorists even have gained notoriety as they participated in daring operations or even rose to leadership roles within their respective terrorist and insurgent organizations. To do this, however, women often have given up their femininity, have been described as "sexless" or "witchy," and have become as hardened operatives as their male colleagues, perhaps in an effort to prove worthy of the terrorist group itself.

On the one hand, one cannot help but respect the efforts of women in terrorist groups in the past as they attempted to compete with men in what must be some of the most difficult circumstances and environments imaginable. Yet, on the other hand, even at their most victorious, these women terrorists only rarely improved the circumstances of their communities or achieved progress towards women's equality in general. More often than not, terrorist leaders utilized the tactical and sometimes strategic advantages produced by having female members without working toward the ideals and goals subscribed to by the women themselves.

Indeed, in a somewhat perverse twist, terrorist leaders apparently have learned that if they deploy women—particularly as couriers and decoys, but also as suicide bombers—they can more easily evade security forces. However, the use of women as logisticians and suicide bombers smacks of exploitation, not achievement. In the past, these women seemed to garner less respect from their male counterparts and were viewed as instruments or tools rather than integral parts of the organization. Similarly, some terrorist leaders cajoled the mothers, sisters, and wives in their societies to encourage young boys and men to become terrorists or even suicide bombers. This cajoling, too, had undertones of exploitation. Implicit in this book, therefore, are a series of tensions revealed as we explored women terrorists, especially as women counterterrorism experts. For one, terrorism in and of itself is horrifying, and yet one curiously identifies with these women as they fight and die for their causes. Additionally, while it is clear that women are not coerced into becoming fighters for the most part, it is also clear that the roles of couriers, decoys, and suicide bombers in particular retain an aspect of exploitation. Although women provide operational benefits to terrorist leaders, their use as suicide bombers and fighters present some downsides, as populations have tended to react negatively to this concept. So it is unclear whether or not the use of female operatives provides greater benefit or cost to terrorist organizations in a general sense. It is also unclear whether being part of a revolutionary group helps the cause of equality for women in socially conservative societies or not.

This final chapter explores general trends in women as terrorists in past and in ongoing conflicts. It also looks forward into the future to consider how the role of women as terrorists might change. To do this, we provide a discussion of overarching trends in the use of women as terrorists. We also present five general findings as scholars, experts, policymakers, and students look to gain greater insight into the role of women as terrorists in the past, present, and future. Finally, we conclude with a section on countering women as terrorists. Although this book is not meant to be a primer on countering terrorism per se, it seems worthwhile to point out the implications of some of our findings for counterterrorism officials in the United States and abroad.

PAST AND PRESENT

In this book, we examined twenty-two different terrorist and insurgent groups that have incorporated women into their day-to-day activities as well as political and military leadership structures. These militant groups range from the Liberation Tigers of Tamil Eelam (LTTE), which at one point controlled significant territory in Sri Lanka with thousands of members and tens of thousands of supporters, to the Japanese Red Army (JRA), which only had an estimated fifty members even at its strongest. We also researched urban-based terrorist groups, such as the Italian Red Brigades, as well as insurgent groups based primarily in rural areas like Sendero Luminoso, or Shining Path, in Peru. Finally, we attempted to include secular militant groups, such as the Baader-Meinhof Gang in Germany (or the Red Army Faction), as well as religiously motivated groups like al-Qa'ida, Lebanese Hizballah, and Palestinian Hamas. All-in-all, we examined the role of women in twenty-two different terrorist and insurgent groups worldwide. In exploring these myriad terrorist and insurgent groups, moreover, we discovered that despite their differences, women seem to play six basic roles: logistician, recruiter, suicide bomber (or martyr), guerrilla fighter, operational leader, or political vanguard.

As a point of departure for this chapter, therefore, Table 7.1 lists the twenty-two various terrorist and insurgent groups in this book. We also list the six different roles that women have played in an effort to compare and contrast these groups against each other.

It is clear from Table 7.1 that terrorist and insurgent groups have mostly utilized women as logisticians in the past. Of the twenty-two terrorist and insurgent groups in our study, twenty-one evidenced women as logisticians. The one exception is the JRA. This particular terrorist group was unique because it had a limited number of members. It also received safe haven in the Lebanese refugee camps along with its Palestinian allies. These two factors probably account for the lack of stories on JRA women logisticians. Otherwise, all of the other groups in our study evidenced the use of women as logisticians, especially if one defines logisticians as including couriers, fundraisers, protectors, and decoys as we did in our chapter. Indeed, even terrorist and insurgent groups in socially conservative communities, which tend to shy away from using women as operatives, rely on women as logisticians. Lebanese Hizballah, for example, has incorporated women's organizations into its fundraising structure and even as protectors. The Groupe Islamique Arme (GIA) in Algeria similarly utilized women as decoys during the Millennium bombing plot. Significantly, our study revealed that women logisticians often risk arrest and death, even though terrorist leaders might see this role as inherently safer than others. Given the preponderance of women logisticians in the past, moreover, we would expect this pattern of terrorist and insurgent leaders' use of women to continue into the future as well.

After logistician, the next most common role for women in our selection of terrorist and insurgent groups is that of political vanguard. We found this discovery to be somewhat surprising. And yet, a thorough

Table 7.1 Women as terrorists: Comparison of twenty-two terrorist groups worldwide

Group	Logistician	Recruiter	Martyr	Guerrilla	Operational Leader	Political Vanguard
al-Aqsa Martyrs' Brigades	X	X	X			
al-Qa'ida Central	X	X				
al-Qa'ida in Iraq	X		X			
Baader-Meinhof Gang[a]	X	X			X	X
Chechen Separatists	X	X	X			
Euskadi Ta Askatasuna	X				X	X
Groupe Islamique Arme	X					
Harakat al-Muqawama al-Islamiyya[b]	X		X			X
Hizballah	X					X
Jemaah Islamiyyah	X					
Japanese Red Army	X				X	X
Liberation Tigers of Tamil Eelam	X	X	X	X		X
Partiya Karkerên Kurdistan[c]	X		X	X		X
Palestinian Islamic Jihad	X		X			
Popular Front for the Liberation of Palestine	X		X		X	
Primea Linea[d]	X				X	X
Provisional Irish Republican Army	X	X			X	X
Red Brigades	X				X	X
Revolutionary Armed Forces of Colombia	X	X		X		
Sandinista National Liberation Front	X			X		X
Sendero Luminoso[e]	X	X		X	X	X
Ejército Zapatista de Liberación Nacional[f]	X			X		X

Groups: [a]Also known as Red Army Faction (RAF); [b]Hamas; [c]Kurdish Workers' Party; [d]Front Line; [e]Shining Path; [f]Zapatista Revolutionary Army.

exploration of women as terrorists reveals that women have taken on the role of political vanguards in half of the terrorist and insurgent groups in our study. Chapter 6 identified three subcategories of political vanguards: strategic visionaries, central committee members, and political officials. Of these three subcategories, women emerged more prominently in the central committees of terrorist and insurgent groups than as strategic visionaries or political officials.

In some cases, these women were responsible for overseeing charitable activities or women's issues in their communities. Rima Fakhry, a central committee member for Hizballah in Lebanon, for example, appeared to have been given this position based on her involvement in Hizballah women's organizations in the past. Several years after her appointment to the central committee, however, it became evident from news reports that her authority and position had expanded over time. Conversely, in other instances, women in central leadership committees oversaw the military operations of their terrorist and insurgent groups. Maria Soledad Iparraguirre Guenechea, a central committee member for Euskadi Ta Askatasuna between 2000 and 2004, for example, had responsibility over military operations. These examples not withstanding, a certain degree of exploitation was present in the relationship between women terrorists and their group leaders in this study. That is, husbands often made wives a part of their central committees, perhaps as a means of ensuring control and loyalty over the central leadership of their terrorist and insurgent groups. Examples of this emerged in the Shining Path in Peru and Partiya Karkerên Kurdistan (PKK; or Kurdish Workers' Party) in Turkey. It also appeared that women sometimes were given a leadership position as a means of appealing to journalists and outside supporters. So it is difficult to argue that just because women hold leadership positions in terrorist and insurgent groups, such as the PKK, Revolutionary Armed Forces of Colombia, or Hizballah, women's status under the rule of such groups would improve in general or even at all.

Interestingly, suicide bombers or "martyrs" and operational leaders were tied for the third most common role of women as terrorists in this book. This observation is also significant, given that terrorists' use of women as suicide bombers does not span the entire three decades of terrorist history. Indeed, of the terrorist and insurgent groups in this study, the first evidence of terrorist leaders' use of female suicide bombers occurred in the early 1990s from the LTTE in Sri Lanka. Of course, it is difficult to interpret terrorist leaders' utilization of women as suicide bombers to be progress in any way. While these leaders for the most part have not brainwashed or coerced women to become suicide bombers, this particular role evidences tinges of exploitation, even more so than with women as political vanguards. One of the most awful stories in this regard is of the Iraqi female suicide bomber Hasna Maryi, who took on this role clearly to follow in her brother's footsteps, yet she was treated with disdain by her male colleagues even at the point of her martyrdom. Thus, as with political vanguards and logisticians, the presence of women as suicide bombers can only be viewed as another form of exploitation by terrorist leaders, even if the individual women themselves are not coerced.

In our analysis of twenty-two different terrorist and insurgent groups, recruiter was the fourth most common role for women. We identified three different sub-categories of recruiter, including facilitators, propagandists, and historical conscience. In this regard, women as propagandists is particularly interesting, because the anonymity of the Internet has enabled women to taken on this role today more than any time. Indeed, this emerging trend appears to be true especially for women supporters of al-Qa'ida, for whom it is clear that al-Qa'ida leadership would rather they remain in the background. Ayman al-Zawahiri (the second in command for al-Qa'ida) stated publicly in January 2008 that women did not have a significant role in the public activities of al-Qa'ida but should quietly suffer and support their male counterparts. Yet the women of al-Qa'ida have used the Internet to contribute, despite this rebuke. It is difficult to interpret the fact that women have attempted to use the Internet to recruit male and female suicide bombers for al-Qa'ida as progress for women in general. Nevertheless, we would consider this development an emerging trend in women as terrorists.

Finally, guerrilla leaders appear to be our least common role for women in terrorist and insurgent groups. In a select few cases, such as with Commandante Ramona for the Zapatista Revolutionary Army in Mexico and Edith Lagos for the Shining Path in Peru, women have become guerrilla fighters and leaders in their own right, but this did not emerge as frequently in our analysis as the other roles. In part, this observation could be the result of our selection of case studies. Of the twenty-two terrorist and insurgent groups in our analysis, arguably only nine have been involved in guerrilla warfare against their respective central governments. That is, slightly less than half of our case studies utilized guerrilla warfare in the first place, so it is perhaps logical that fewer women as guerrilla fighters would emerge in our analysis. Indeed, of the nine terrorist and insurgent groups in our analysis that adopted guerrilla warfare activities, six utilized women in these struggles. Three did not: al-Qa'ida in Iraq (AQI), Lebanese Hizballah, and the GIA in Algeria. A more expansive study might actually find this role to be as important as the others. Nonetheless, on the basis of the past record, we do not anticipate that other ongoing insurgencies, such as the Taliban, will begin to utilize women as guerrilla fighters extensively in the future.

Of course, the past is not always a good predictor of the future. These previous paragraphs provide some insight into how terrorist and insurgent leaders have utilized women in the past, but are there new ways to think about the role of women in the future? Alternatively, what insights can be gained by this study into how terrorist groups make decisions and why individuals choose to become terrorists in the first place? The following sections provide some more general findings that we thought would be of interest to terrorism experts, policymakers, and even wider audiences.

FUTURE

Having conducted research on terrorism for a number of years, we were certainly surprised at how much insight into terrorist group dynamics could be derived from a study of women as terrorists. One of the most striking themes throughout the previous chapters is the observation that terrorist leaders think about the female cadré differently than their male counterparts. The calculation undertaken by terrorist leaders on how to deploy their female members was sometimes strategic and other times opportunistic, but it was consistently different. Moreover, the difference in calculation appears to have revolved around three basic factors: propaganda value, effectiveness, and community backlash. Terrorist leaders weighted the propaganda value of women members and their ability to elude security officials against the potential backlash from support communities.

For example, in the case of LTTE's use of a female suicide bomber, Thenmuli Rajaratnam, to assassinate Rajiv Gandhi, the former Prime Minister of India, clearly demonstrated strategic thinking on the part of LTTE leadership and operational planners. One can imagine them thinking, how can we get close enough to assassinate Gandhi? A woman was the logical conclusion: she was more likely to get near Gandhi by providing him with a garland than a man. Thus, a woman was chosen for the attack. Thenmuli Rajaratnam clearly was not chosen, over any given male suicide bomber, based on merit or even perhaps eagerness, but simply because of her gender. One could also imagine that LTTE leaders initially were concerned about the potential backlash in Tamil society for their use of a female suicide bomber. Addressing this concern, the story was put out—whether true or not—that Thenmuli Rajaratnam had been repeatedly raped and wanted to conduct the attack to redeem herself. Again, this story would not have been necessary with a male suicide bomber, demonstrating a certain extra calculus undertaken by the LTTE leadership in considering this particular attack.

The same could be said for the case of Ahlam Tamimi, who acted as decoy for a Palestinian male suicide bomber in the August 2001 attack against the Sbarro Pizza restaurant in downtown Jerusalem. Published interviews with Tamimi indicate that she was chosen as decoy because her gender made her much less suspicious than a man. In fact, Palestinian terrorist leaders made the calculation that a male–female team would be less suspicious than just a male suicide bomber on his own. This calculation suggests strategic thinking on the part of terrorist leaders, not just for the target selected but also for the personnel involved in the attack.

In comparison, the example of women suicide bombers for the Kurdish terrorist group in Turkey, PKK, indicates more opportunistic thinking. And yet even thinking opportunistically, PKK leaders still used a different calculus in their deployment of women, as opposed to men. Recall that women originally fought side-by-side with men as guerrilla fighters, until they experienced harassment at the hands of their male comrades. Thus, PKK leaders separated women fighters from the men, opening the door for female fighters to volunteer for suicide missions. One can almost imagine PKK leaders thinking, "Okay, let's give it a shot." Once the attacks by female suicide operatives proved successful, the tactic was incorporated into the PKK operational mindset.

Suicide terrorism, of course, is always shocking and horrific. Yet Palestinian terrorist groups, AQI, and the Chechen separatist groups appear to have used women as bombers specifically to magnify this horror. In the same way, the fact that women were willing to take on a role traditionally held by men in the terrorist groups—especially in conservative societies—also served to motivate men to volunteer as well. It seemed almost as if terrorist leaders used women for the shock factor, not doubt, but also to shame their male counterparts into greater loyalty. Indeed, this calculation could also be seen in the role of women as political vanguards. Terrorist groups, like al-Qa'ida, have begun to use their women supporters in a more public way, partially as a means of shaming their fathers, brothers, and husbands into taking on a more significant role in the fight. Perhaps this preference is the result of male domination, but it also could simply be part of an inherent cost–benefit analysis: female suicide bombers might be able to distract security officials, but male suicide operatives do not risk the same backlash in the terrorists' support community. In this sense, it is almost as if the terrorist leaders would *prefer* more male cadres, but they will assume more risk and use women if necessary.

We also learned, during the course of researching and writing this book, that female terrorists, like women everywhere, have fought for the right to play a significant role in terrorist groups. This battle for respect and equality is another striking theme throughout the chapters in this book, whether it be the creation of an al-Qa'ida–affiliated magazine aimed at women or the establishment of women's branches in the Provisional Irish Republican Army (PIRA), women have attempted to carve out a space for themselves within terrorist organizational structures. In some instances, terrorist leaders have taken advantage of this desire for respect and equality on the part of women cadre and supporters, but in other instances they did not.

For example, Leila Khaled's autobiography states that she deserted Fatah and joined with the Popular Front for the Liberation of Palestine–GC (PFLP-GC) because the latter would let her take on the role of guerrilla fighter and operative, as opposed to fundraiser. According to Khaled, most Palestinian women were willing to accept roles as fundraisers and perhaps logisticians; however, she was not, and she could not find space for herself and women fighters within the structure and internal dynamics of Fatah. Indeed, Khaled's story suggests that Fatah leaders were not willing to risk societal backlash or did not think that women fighters would be effective.

Recall a similar story told by a female PIRA explosives expert in Chapter 2. She might have been a top explosives expert at the time of her interview with Eileen Fairweather and the other authors of *Only the Rivers Run Free*, but that particular female PIRA volunteer progressed over time from courier and scout to bomb maker and instructor. This interview can be interpreted in a number of ways. Some might read it and believe that the PIRA allowed women to be promoted easily within their ranks. Perhaps, but a more interesting conclusion, in this context, is that the interviewee worked for her promotions within the PIRA, building rapport with her male counterparts so that she would be trusted. Therefore, one can imagine that she was able to successfully create space for herself within the PIRA as a bomb maker, but the responsibility did not come easily to her as she struggled to receive recognition and promotion.

One might expect that this struggle by women terrorists for respect and recognition would be more pronounced in conservative societies that in more progressive—at least in the terms of equality for women—societies in western Europe. This appears to be true when it comes to women in leadership positions within terrorist organizations. Yet many terrorist groups operating in more conservative societies (e.g., Peru, Colombia, or Sri Lanka) had at least as high or sometimes a higher proportion of women fighters than their Western European counterparts.

Perhaps a better division, given a post-9/11 world, would be religious versus predominantly secular terrorist groups. This avenue clearly needs further exploration. It is also possible that the calculation made by terrorist leaders—propaganda, effectiveness, and backlash—might be weighted differently than counterterrorism officials expect. That is, certainly the backlash from supporters in a more conservative society would be higher, but so too could effectiveness.

Additionally, it seems clear that women terrorists have been able to expand their respective terrorist and insurgent groups' operational capabilities. This observation is particularly true in societies where security authorities do not expect women to be directly involved in violent acts or are limited in their abilities to search women closely. The participation of the Chechen Black Widows in the October 2002 Moscow theater hostage-taking allowed the Chechen insurgents to carry out this operation because they were able to enter the theater concealing bombs undetected by authorities. This attack, although ultimately disrupted by Russian special forces, allowed the Chechen militants to stage a sophisticated operation in which they took 850 hostages for two and a half days, something that without the participation of the 19 women, they may not have been able to accomplish. Similarly, the other examples such as the use of female suicide bombers by AQI, female decoys by the PIRA, and money smugglers by Palestinian terrorists all suggest that utilizing women operatives can help improve the overall viability and capabilities of a militant organization.

For most terrorist and insurgent groups, whether religious or secular, the decision to use women to carry out violent acts is a pragmatic choice rather than because a group's ideology or dogma dictated that women should be included or out of concern for the equal rights of women. Women's involvement in terrorist attacks is typically not expected by security services or the public because women are not traditionally associated with promulgating violence, but rather protecting the innocent— primarily children—from becoming victims of violence. As we have discovered in our research, this commonly held assumption is not necessarily accurate, particularly when it comes to societies engaged in civil war or who are experiencing significant internal conflict. If women in a conflict are motivated to become part of the militant movement and/or the militant movement sees a clear-cut way that by allowing women to participate in operations, they can expand their target set, maintain the group's viability, bring media attention to their cause, and make advancements against the adversary, then this is often when women are most likely to make a more direct contribution to the violence.

Despite the operational contributions that women have made, particularly in recent years, the role that women have played behind the scenes has been largely discounted by both the men in these militant groups and the researchers who have studied them. Although women who support the men in the field (e.g., by passing messages, smuggling weapons, and providing cover and shelter) are performing tasks that are not very glamorous, without their contribution, more men would have to step in and perform these necessary functions, thus taking more men out of combat and forcing them to diversify in order to sustain the group. Moreover, without women to protect the men involved in planning and executing operations, evidence suggests that male operatives would suffer more vulnerability to detection by security services.

In addition to the everyday support that women provide their men—husbands, brothers, in-laws, sons, and fathers—they also serve as the primary educators of their society's children. As such, they pass along the mores, values, culture, biases, anger, and frustration that their families and friends have experienced in their history at the hands of whomever they are fighting against. We have seen the image time and again of the Palestinian mother, who speaks of her pride at the loss of her son or daughter to a martyrdom operation. These messages that mothers, who in many conflict-ridden societies are the dominant presence in the home, send to their children that an eye for an eye is acceptable, that it is permissible to kill innocent civilians to exact revenge for perceived grievances against the state or its people, and that it is better to die young for a cause rather than live and try to change things through peace and understanding all have a tremendous impact on future generations and further entrench the conflict in these areas for years to come.

Finally, our research on women as terrorists also reflected a certain bias in the counterterrorism expert community to focus on terrorist leadership and operatives. This bias tends to underemphasize the role of women in terrorist groups. We are not necessarily arguing that women terrorists should be an important focus of counterterrorism activities or even academic research, but women often are ignored in the study of social phenomena. The same has been true of women who have played a role in terrorist groups, not as fighters or operatives, but as political vanguards, logisticians, and recruiters. These behind-the-scenes activities, however, can be essential for the terrorist group in order to sustain its violent activities as well as its wider support base and so should not be dismissed.

Take, for example, the role that PIRA women played in the hunger strikes to build morale and keep unity among the Republican community. Palestinian women played a similar role during the 1987 Intifada in the West Bank and Gaza Strip. Thus, the responsibility that women take on as "protectors" could be viewed as key to the success of any given terrorist movement. We also learned that despite the fact that there do not appear to be many female recruiters occupying formal leadership positions in which they are responsible for a militant group's membership, women recruit new terrorists in many different ways: by grooming the next generation of terrorists through recounting stories of victimization and grievances, by encouraging family members and friends to offer themselves up to the resistance, and as examples of martyrdom themselves.

Despite examples of women in leadership positions in the 1960s and 1970s who were able to assert their influence and ideas over the strategic direction of their particular group, few women today occupy these same positions or maintain this same kind of power within a militant group. There are several explanations for this: the fact that the ideology of the groups that fronted women as leaders was based on a more egalitarian model and is no longer an ideology that has much traction outside of a few parts of the world; that more groups engaged in terrorist violence today, whether secular or religious, have a more socially conservative outlook and thus do not see women as occupying politically influential positions with decision-making power; and that where deployed, women are being largely used as propaganda for their respective groups. Although it may appear on the surface that women are gaining influence through their direct involvement in violent operations, most groups do not see this as a stepping stone to deeper involvement in the leadership cadre of their organizations. Indeed, in most of the terrorist and insurgent groups that we examined, the strategic decision-making roles were still reserved for men. Perhaps women's increasing involvement in violent operations portends, or is the first step toward, greater involvement in the leadership cadre of some militant groups. However, it seems more likely that women will continue to play critical behind-the-scenes roles that will enable the militant groups' continued existence, through enabling communication, operations, and sustaining the family and friendship networks that keep the conflict going and feed the resistance.

COUNTERING WOMEN AS TERRORISTS

In writing this book, it was our intention to provide a thorough look at the motivations, roles, and activities undertaken by women as terrorists throughout history. Rather than focusing on a particular country or terrorist group, therefore, we chose to examine myriad different clandestine organizations and structured the book according to the roles that women have assumed in the past. We hoped that this structure would provided greater insight into women as terrorists, but also into the key positions that terrorist and insurgent groups have utilized to sustain a violent campaign over time, regardless of whether these positions were filled by men or by women. Perhaps one of the more interesting findings was a tendency for journalists, historians, policy analysts, and policymakers to focus on terrorist leaders and operatives, rather than the support networks that surround clandestine groups. This emphasis, it seems to us, underestimates the importance of support networks—and women—to the overall success of a terrorist campaign. Nonetheless, our research also had some implications for counterterrorism policymakers. We, thus, determined to add a brief section at the conclusion of this book to highlight some of the more worthwhile implications.

First, terrorist experts and intelligence officials alike tend to view the use of women by terrorist leaders, particularly for suicide missions, as a sign of desperation. That is, once a particular terrorist or insurgent group begins to utilize women suicide bombers, this shift is taken to mean that they are under significant pressure from counterterrorism activities: the counterterrorism strategy is working. In many ways, this interpretation of events makes sense. It is arguable, for example, that AQI only turned to female suicide bombers when times were rough with the United States–led surge in 2007 and the Iraqi-led Awakening Movement in al-Anbar Province. Similarly, at first glance, the al-Aqsa Martyrs' Brigades in the West Bank and Gaza Strip apparently adopted this tactic because it had difficulty attracting male suicide bombers.

Despite its logic, our findings suggest that this "sign of desperation" conclusion is an over-generalization. Shifts in the behavior and decision making of terrorist leaders, of course, provide important insight into the status of a particular terrorist or insurgent group. Nonetheless, our research revealed that terrorist leaders' adoption of women for typically male-dominated tasks could be signs of something beyond desperation. For example, the adoption of women in this way could simply be the result of a tactical shift made by terrorist leaders in response to a counterterrorism measure implemented by security forces. Along the lines of "let's try this and see what happens," the utilization of women as logisticians and suicide bombers in these circumstances would be less a sign of desperation than of tactical creativity. That is, it would be difficult to argue that the LTTE and PKK adopted women as recruiters and suicide bombers out of desperation, contradicting the pattern observed in AQI and al-Aqsa Martyrs' Brigades. It seems more likely the use of women as terrorists by the LTTE in Sri Lanka and PKK in Turkey reinforces our understanding of them as tactically innovative, rather than desperate. The implication of this alternative explanation is for counterterrorism and homeland security officials to pay close attention to terrorist and insurgent groups that begin to utilize women, because they could make additional tactical innovations in the future.

Beyond a sign of tactical innovation, terrorist leaders' adoption of women for roles typically filled by men also could be a sign of internal pressure within the terrorist group itself or the support population. It seems clear from stories of the hunger strike in 1981 that the PIRA in Northern Ireland capitulated to pressure from within the organization and perhaps even its support population to utilize women more and more. PIRA leaders initially did not want women to participate in the hunger strikes, but acceded to the wishes of women prisoners, especially because they drew significant media attention. A similar argument could be made for Lebanese Hizballah and the placement of a woman onto its political committee, although that pressure only began to yield results thirty years after the birth of Hizballah. In these circumstances, it would be wrong to view the adoption of women by terrorist leaders as a sign of desperation, but more like innovation, which suggests that the leaders of these particular terrorist and insurgent groups were willing to adjust their behavior in order to keep their members and support populations happy. That is, the use of women in these instances was a sign of sensitivity to support populations, rather than a sign of desperation. These two alternative explanations—innovation and sensitivity to support populations—would be worthwhile for terrorism experts and intelligence analysts to consider as they assess the emergence of women terrorists in the future.

Second, security forces historically have struggled to intercept women terrorists, especially logisticians and suicide bombers. Women have utilized sexual advances, faked pregnancies, and used baby carriages, veils, and religious clothing, among other things, to slip past security barriers. This struggle on the part of security forces is not unique to the Muslim world and U.S. forces in Iraq. Indeed, recall that Eileen MacDonald's 1991 book on women terrorists was titled *Shoot the Women First*; this title was taken from a conversation she had with German security officials. Security forces have attempted to resolve this dilemma in a number of ways.

In Sri Lanka, for example, efforts are made to not simply intercept suicide bombers themselves, but the support cells surrounding these individuals. This approach presents multiple opportunities for interception, rather than simply at the point of denotation for a suicide bomber and reduces the possibility that a woman in particular might slip through security checkpoints. Alternatively, security forces in the Middle East, such as Jordan and more recently Iraq, have begun to use women officers to observe and check potential female terrorists at checkpoints. The logic behind this approach is that women are less inhibited to thoroughly check and frisk other women for suicide vests or other hidden devices. In Iraq the program is titled Daughters of Iraq, and it pays approximately US$300 per month.[1] Finally, it is not uncommon for young, single women to be separated out for intensive questioning at airports, in part because examples exist of women being used as unsuspecting bomb couriers in the past.

In addition to these tactical counterterrorism techniques, the exploitation of women by terrorist leaders presents an opportunity for counterterrorism policy. That is, "hearts and minds" activities tend to focus on potential male recruits for terrorist groups, but what about their female counterparts? For example, well-known Salafi ideologues, such as Dr. Fadl, have begun to criticize al-Qa'ida from a theological perspective.[2] Preliminary evidence suggests that these criticisms might have an impact on male recruits, but it is unclear whether female recruits would respond similarly to theological arguments. Perhaps well-known women leaders of nongovernmental organizations or journalists would present different and more persuasive arguments to women terrorists. Similarly, although it is easy to focus on programs to dissuade suicide bombers, women play an equally important role as logisticians and recruiters. It would be worth exploring the possibility of developing programs and activities to persuade mothers, sisters, and wives that the men in their family should not join terrorist groups or, alternatively, that becoming a courier is not a worthwhile pursuit. In Israel, for example, security authorities sometimes demolish the homes of suicide bombers. The purpose of these demolitions is to dissuade subsequent recruits from becoming suicide bombers, because their families will suffer. Although we do not advocate home demolitions, the logic behind this counterterrorism tactic—dissuading the families of would-be suicide bombers—appears valid and therefore worth exploring further.

In conclusion, it is not our intention to argue that the increasing prominence of women as terrorists in the world represents a new or significant threat to security. In many instances, it seems clear that terrorist leaders simply view women logisticians, recruiters, and suicide bombers as additional weapons in their arsenal. The emergence of women as political vanguards is perhaps more interesting, because it suggests that some terrorist leaders believe that these women can appeal to wider audiences for support and sympathy. Nonetheless, in looking at terrorism through the lens of female operatives, we found that this lens provides insight into gaps in our knowledge and understanding of the general phenomenon. In particular, the support networks that sustain terrorist and insurgent groups appear to be understudied and less understood than their operational leaders and tactics. Yet this book underscores that other tasks, such as couriers, decoys, protectors, fund-raisers, propagandists, and historical conscience, can be equally important for terrorist and insurgent groups. In ignoring these roles, we underestimate the contribution that women have made to terrorist groups, but, perhaps more importantly, we also overlook opportunities to reduce the threat that terrorism poses to innocent civilians around the world, regardless of gender.

Notes

Chapter 1

1. Eileen MacDonald, *Shoot the Women First* (London: Fourth Estate, 1991), 4.

2. Eileen MacDonald similarly writes about an interview with Scotland Yard, in which they stated that the primary difference between female and male terrorists was women's ability to use their "feminine wiles" against the arresting officers. Ibid., 5.

3. Walter Laqueur, *The Age of Terrorism,* 2nd ed. (Boston: Little, Brown and Co, 1987), 11.

4. Laqueur, *The Age of Terrorism*, 145.

5. At a conference sponsored by the Brookings Institution in July 2003, Francis Fukuyama argued, for example, that terrorism studies are irrelevant to the discipline of international relations without a considerable focus on state-sponsored terrorism.

6. Although released in 2001, J. Bowyer Bell conducted most of his research on terrorism in the 1980s and early 1990s. In many ways, this book was a reissue of previous work. It represented a mindset that the discipline will never reach an agreed-upon understanding of what, exactly, constitutes terrorism. J. Bowyer Bell, *The IRA 1968–2000: An Analysis of a Secret Army* (London: Frank Cass, 2001), 6.

7. According to lore in the terrorism community, this statement was first made at a conference in the mid-1970s by J. Bowyer Bell. Its great proponent in the U.S. counterterrorism community, however, has been Brian Jenkins.

8. For further discussion in the U.S. government's approach to terrorism and how this has evolved, see David Tucker, *Skirmishes at the Edge of Empire* (Westport: Praeger, 1997).

9. David Rapoport, ed., *Inside Terrorist Organizations* (London: Frank Cass, 1988), 1.

10. Ibid., 1.

11. Martha Crenshaw, "Theories of Terrorism," in Rapoport, 3.

12. The Gush Emunim was a Jewish religious terrorist organization that operated in the West Bank in the mid-1980s. Ehud Sprinzak, *Brother Against Brother* (New York: Free Press, 1999).

13. *Terrorism and Violence* is edited by David Rapoport; the other journal *Political Conflict and Terrorism* is edited by Bruce Hoffman.

14. Ehud Sprinzak, "The Process of Delegitimation: Towards a Linkage Theory of Political Terrorism," *Terrorism and Violence* 3, no. 1 (Spring 1991), 52.

15. Ibid., 52.

16. Donatella della Porta, "Left-wing Terrorism in Italy," in *Terrorism in Context*, ed. Martha Crenshaw (University Park, PA: Pennsylvania State University Press, 2001), 105–159.

17. Ibid., 105–159.

18. Bruce Hoffman, *Inside Terrorism* (New York City: Columbia University Press, 1998), 162.

19. See, for example, John Esposito, *Holy War: Terror in the Name of Islam* (Oxford: Oxford University Press, 2002).

20. Mark Juergensmeyer, *Terror in the Mind of God: The Global Rise of Religious Violence* (Berkeley: University of California Press, 2001).

21. Ibid., 160–62.

22. See, for example, J. Ross, "Structural Causes of Oppositional Political Terrorism: Towards a Causal Model," *Journal of Peace Research* 3 (1993): 317–29.

23. See, for example, Marc Sageman, *Understanding Terrorist Networks* (Philadelphia: University of Pennsylvania Press, 2004), 138–74.

24. Kim Cragin and Scott Gerwehr, *Dissuading Terror: Strategic Influence and the Struggle against Terrorism* (Santa Monica, CA: RAND Corporation, 2005).

25. Usama bin Laden, "Declaration of Jihad," in *Messages to the World: The Statements of Osama bin Laden,* ed. Bruce Lawrence (London: Verso, 2005), 25.

26. Ibid., 50.

27. Ibid., 51.

28. Kevin Bohn, "Virginia Jihad Suspects Charged with Plotting to Fight US," *CNN,* 26 (September 2003), http://www.cnn.com/2003/LAW/09/25/virginia.terror.suspects (accessed 25 August 2007).

29. Carrie Hamilton, "Re-membering the Basque Nationalist Family: Daughters, Fathers and the Reproduction of the Radical Nationalist Community," *Journal of Spanish Cultural Studies,* 1, no. 2 (September 2000), 160.

30. Ibid., 162–63.

31. MacDonald, *Shoot the Women First,* 20–21.

32. Clark McCauley, "Psychological Issues in Understanding Terrorism and the Response to Terrorism," in *The Psychology of Terrorism,* ed. Christopher Stout (Westport, CT: Greenwood, forthcoming).

33. See Crenshaw, *Terrorism in Context,* 105–59.

34. Sageman, *Understanding Terrorist Networks.*

35. For more information, see Kim Hyun Hui, *Tears of My Soul* (London: William Morrow & Co., 1993).

36. *Five Letters to the African Corps,* September 1993–May 1994, U.S. military document number AF GP-2002-600053, http://cisac.stanford.edu/publications/harmony_and_disharmony_exploiting_alqaidas_organizational_vulnerabilities (accessed 2 February 2009).

37. *Five Letters to the African Corps.*

38. R. Kim Cragin, "Early History of al-Qaida," *The Historial Journal*, 51, no. 4 (2008), 1047–67.

39. Kim Cragin, "Hizballah, Party of God," in *Aptitude for Destruction,* ed. Brian Jackson et al. (Santa Monica: RAND Corporation, 2005), 45.

40. For more information, see Kim Cragin et al., *Sharing the Dragon's Teeth: Terrorist Groups' Exchange of Technologies and Knowledge* (Santa Monica: RAND Corporation, 2007).

41. Author interviews, Singhalese security officials, Colombo, Sri Lanka, February 2003.

42. For more information, see Chapter 2 "Women as Logisticians."

43. Ibid.

44. Menachem Levi quoted in Ehud Sprinzak, *Brother Against Brother* (New York: The Free Press, 1999), 158.

Chapter 2

1. Definition available online at Merriam-Webster Online Dictionary, http://www.merriam-webster.com/dictionary/logistics (accessed 11 November 2008).

2. Leila Khaled, *My People Shall Live: An Autobiography of a Revolutionary,* trans. George Hajjar (London: Hodder and Stoughton, 1973), 105.

3. Ibid., 119.

4. See, for example, stories told by women terrorists in Barbara Victor, *Army of Roses: Inside the World of Palestinian Women Suicide Bombers* (New York: Rodale, 2003); and Eileen Fairweather et al., *Only the Rivers Run Free: Northern Ireland: The Women's War* (London: Pluto Press, 1984).

5. Karla Cunningham, "Cross-Regional Trends in Female Terrorism," *Studies in Conflict and Terrorism* 26 (2003): 174, cited in Jeffrey Louis Decker, "Terrorism (Un)Veiled: Frantz Fanon and the Women of Algiers," *Cultural Critique* 17 (Winter 1990): 190–92.

6. Rhinnian Talbot, "Myths in the Representation of Women Terrorists," *Eire-Ireland* (Fall 2001): 7.

7. Amira Hass, *Drinking the Sea at Gaza: Days and Nights in a Land Under Seige* (New York: Henry Holt and Company, 1999), 42.

8. Joost Hilterman, "Trade Unions and Women's Committees: Sustaining Movement, Creating Space," *Middle East Report,* May/August 1990, 32–36; Rema Hammimi, "Women, the Hijab and the Uprising," *Middle East Report,* May/August 1990, 24–28.

9. "Leaflet No. 6," reprinted in Shaul Mishal and Reuben Aharoni, *Speaking Stones: Communiqués from the Intifada Underground* (Syracuse, NY: Syracuse University Press, 1994), 64.

10. Ibid.

11. Ibid., 67.

12. Barbara Victor, *Army of Roses: Inside the World of Palestinian Women Suicide Bombers*, (New York: Rodale, 2003), 268.

13. Ibid.

14. Cunningham, "Cross-Regional Trends in Female Terrorism," 177.

15. Ibid.

16. Al-Jazeerah produced an "Every Woman" special entitled, "Women of Hizballah" in December 2006. This video can be found on YouTube at http://www.youtube.com/watch?v=P2QaqseIGv8 (accessed 20 October 2008).

17. Fairweather et al., *Only the Rivers Run Free*, 207.

18. Ibid., 250.

19. Ibid., 242.

20. Jeremy McDermott, "Colombia Extradites Rebel 'Sonia,'" *BBC News*, 9 March 2005, http://news.bbc.co.uk/2/hi/americas/4331673.stm (accessed 12 July 2007).

21. "The Guerrilla Sonia," an interview posted in January 2005, http://www.pachakuti.org/textos/hemeroteca/2005_1/prisioneros5.htm (12 November 2007).

22. "Morocco Uncovers al-Qaeda Plot," *BBC News*, 11 June 2002, http://news.bbc.co.uk/2/hi/africa/2037391.stm (accessed 10 October 2008).

23. "CIA Helps Defuse al-Qaeda Bomb Plot in Morocco," *CNN News*, 16 June 2002, http://archives.cnn.com/2002/WORLD/africa/06/16/terror.arrests/index.html (accessed 10 October 2008).

24. Ibid.

25. Peter Finn, "Al-Qaeda Deputies Harbored by Iran," *Washington Post*, 28 August 2002, A01.

26. Ibid.

27. "Al-Zawahiri: No Women in Al-Qa'ida Ranks," *CBS News*, 22 April 2008, http://www.cbsnews.com/stories/2008/04/22/cbsnews_investigates/main4033865.shtml (accessed 10 October 2008).

28. Marianne Torres, "Women in the Intifada," *Palestine Papers*, August 1989, http://www.sonomacountyfreepress.com/palestine/women2.html (accessed 30 November 2007).

29. Ibid.

30. Naila Daniel, "Palestinian Women in the Intifada," *Peace Magazine*, 13, no. 4 (July-August 1997).

31. Ibid.

32. Ibid.

33. Fairweather et al., *Only the Rivers Run Free*, 50.

34. Ibid.

35. Ibid., 227.

36. Christopher Dickey, "Women of al-Qaeda," *Newsweek*, 12 December 2005.

37. "Jemaah Islamiyyah: Damaged but Still Dangerous," *Asia Report No. 63*, August 2003.

38. Jennifer Koons, "Al-Qaeda in Iraq—Down but not Out," *Iraqi Crisis Report*, No. 266, 25 July 2008, http://www.iwpr.net/index.php?apc_state=hen&s=o&o=l=EN&p=icr&s=f&o=345878 (accessed 10 October 2008).

39. Victor, *Army of Roses*, 142–44.

40. Ibid., 144.

41. See also, "The Role of Palestinian Women in Suicide Terrorism," Israeli Ministry of Foreign Affairs, January 2003, http://www.mfa.gov.il/MFA/MFA Archive/2000_2009/2003/1/The+Role+of+Palestinian+Women+in+Suicide+ Terrorism.htm (accessed 3 June 2006).

42. Ibid.

43. Eileen MacDonald, *Shoot the Women First* (London: Fourth Estate, 1991), 135.

44. Ibid., 208.

45. Ibid., 135.

46. Cunningham, "Cross-Regional Trends in Female Terrorism," 173.

47. Johanna McGeary, "New Year's Evil," *Time*, 26 December 1999, http://www.time.com/time/magazine/article/0,9171,36512-1,00.html (accessed 23 June 2007).

48. "FBI Terrorism Swoop," *BBC News*, 30 December 1999, http://news.bbc.co.uk/1/hi/world/americas/584144.stm (accessed 30 October 2007).

49. "Mauritanian police say mastermind behind the Christmas Eve killings of French tourists arrested," *Associated Press*, 10 April 2008, http://www.iht.com/articles/ap/2008/04/10/africa/AF-GEN-Mauritania-Tourist-Killings.php (accessed 10 October 2008).

Chapter 3

1. Craig Smith, "Police Try to Fathom Belgian Path to Terror," *International Herald Tribune*, 6 December 2005.

2. Edwin Bakker, *Jihadists in Europe—Their Characteristics and the Circumstances in which They Joined the Jihad: An Exploratory Study* (Clingendael: Netherlands Institute of International Relations, 2006).

3. "Treasury Designates Members of Abu Ghadiyah's Network Facilitates flow of terrorists, weapons, and money from Syria to al Qaida in Iraq," press release, 28 February 2008, http://www.ustreas.gov/press/releases/hp845.htm (accessed 20 October 2008).

4. Steven Emerson, *American Jihad: The Terrorists Living Among Us* (New York: Free Press, 2002), 32.

5. Amy Caiazza, "Why Gender Matters in Understanding September 11: Women, Militarism, and Violence," Briefing Paper, Institute for Women's Policy Research, November 2001, http://www.iwpr.org/pdf/terrorism.pdf (accessed 2 February 2009).

6. Sharon Behn, "Female bombers spreading more terror," The Washington Times, 20 March 2008, http://www.washingtontimes.com/apps/pbcs.dll/article?AID=/20080320/FOREIGN/373394613 (accessed 2 February 2009).

7. Gustavo Gorriti, *The Shining Path: A History of the Millenarian War in Peru*, trans. Robin Kirk (Chapel Hill, NC: University of North Carolina Press, 1999).

8. Nathanial C. Nash, "Lima Journal: Shining Path Women: So Many and So Ferocious," *The New York Times*, 22 September 1992.

9. "You'll Learn Not to Cry: Child Combatants in Colombia," *Human Rights Watch Report* (New York: Human Rights Watch, September 2003), 45.

10. "Palestinian 'Targeted Hospital,'" *BBC News,* 21 June 2005, http://news.bbc.co.uk/2/hi/middle_east/4113538.stm (accessed 3 November 2008).

11. Yoram Schweitzer, ed. *Female Suicide Terrorists* (Tel Aviv: Jaffe Center for Strategic Studies, 2003), 38.

12. Kim Murphy, "Black Widows Caught in Web of Chechen War," *LA Times,* 7 February 2004.

13. Karla Cunningham, "Countering Female Terrorism," *Studies in Conflict and Terrorism*, 30, no. 2 (1 February 2007), 119.

14. Ibid.

15. This study was cited in Paige Whaley Eager, *From Freedom Fighters to Terrorists: Women and Political Violence* (New York: Ashgate Publishing, 2008), 148; see also Eileen MacDonald, *Shoot the Women First* (London: Fourth Estate, 1991), 20–21.

16. Kim Jordan and Miram Denov, "Birds of Freedom? Perspectives on Female Emancipation and the Liberation Tigers of Tamil Eelam," *Journal of International Women's Studies*, 9, no. 1 (November 2007), 52.

17. "Suicide Bomber's Widow Soldiers On," *CNN*, 24 August 2006, http://edition.cnn.com/2006/WORLD/asiapcf/08/15/elaroud/index.html (accessed 5 November 2008).

18. Elaine Sciolino and Souad Mekhennet, "Belgian Woman Wages War for Al-Qaeda on the Web," *The International Herald Tribune,* 27 May 2008.

19. Karla Cunningham, "Countering Female Terrorism," *Studies in Conflict and Terrorism* 30, no. 2 (1 February 2007), 114.

20. Ibid., 115.

21. Ibid.

22. Ibid., 121.

23. Leela Jacinto, "Al-Qaeda's 'Female Squads' Go Online," ABC News.com, 23 September 2004, http://abcnews.go.com/International/story?id=84585&page=1; "Al-Qaeda's Women's Magazine: Women Must Participate in Jihad," Special Dispatch Series No. 779, 7 September 2004, http://memri.org/bin/articles.cgi?Page=archives&Area=sd&ID=SP77904#_edn1 (accessed 2 February 2009).

24. Ibid.

25. Farhana Ali, "Ready to Detonate: The Diverse Profiles of Female Suicide Bombers," *The MIPT Terrorism Annual* (November 2006): 49–58.

26. Ibid.

27. Valerie Morgan, "Peacemakers? Peacekeepers? Women in Northern Ireland 1969–1995," A Professorial Lecture Given at the University of Ulster, 25 October 1995, http://cain.ulst.ac.uk/issues/women/paper3.htm (accessed 2 February 2009).

28. Caiazza, "Why Gender Matters in Understanding September 11: Women, Militarism, and Violence."

29. Article 16, reprinted in Mohammad Maqdsi, trans., "The Charter of the Islamic Resistance Movement," *Journal of Palestine Studies* 22 (Spring 1993), 122–34.

30. Ibid.

31. Evgenii Novikov, "The Recruiting and Organizational Structure of Hizb ut-Tahrir," *Terrorism Monitor* 2, no. 22, The Jamestown Foundation, 18 November 2004, http://www.jamestown.org/publications_details.php?volume_id=400 &issue_id=3148&article_id=2368890.

32. Mohammed Hafez, "Manufacturing Human Bombs: Strategy, Culture, and Conflict in the Making of Palestinian Suicide Bombers," United States Institute of Peace, 4 April 2005.

33. The Muslim *Khilafa* is the successor to the Prophet Mohammed as the political, military, and administrative leader of the Muslims. He would preside over the Muslim Caliphate, which is an Islamic form of government that represents the unity of the Muslim world.

34. Evgenii Novikov, "The Recruiting and Organizational Structure of Hizb ut-Tahrir," *Terrorism Monitor* 2, no. 22, The Jamestown Foundation, 18 November 2004, http://www.jamestown.org/publications_details.php?volume_id=400 &issue_id=3148&article_id=2368890.

Chapter 4

1. For more information on the Black Widows and Chechen militants see, Steven Lee Myers, "From Dismal Chechnya, Women Turn to Bombs," *New York Times,* 10 September 2004; Anne Speckhard and Khapta Ahkmedova, "The Making of a Martyr: Chechen Suicide Terrorism," *Studies in Conflict and Terrorism* 29, no. 5, (August 2006), 429–92; and Anne Speckhard and Khapta Akhmedova, "Black Widows: The Chechen Female Suicide Terrorists," in *Female Suicide Terrorists,* ed. Yoram Schweitzer (Tel Aviv: Jaffe Center for Strategic Studies, 2006).

2. For more information on women fighters for the LTTE, see the LTTE Web site, www.tamilnation.org (accessed 4 September 2007). See also "Women Tiger Rebels Shot in Sri Lanka after Prince Charles Visit," Agence France Presse, 28 February 2005; "Tamil Tigers Mark Anniversary of First Suicide Attack," Agence France Presse, 5 July 2005.

3. For more information on Palestinian women fighters, see Mira Tzoreff, "The Palestinian Shahida," in *Female Suicide Terrorists,* ed. Yoram Schweitzer (Tel Aviv: Jaffe Center for Strategic Studies 2003); Barbara Victor, *Army of Roses: Inside the World of Palestinian Women Suicide Bombers* (New York: Rodale, 2003); and Cameron W. Barr, "Why a Palestinian Girl Now Wants to Be a Suicide Bomber," *Christian Science Monitor,* 1 April 2002, 7.

4. Yoram Schweitzer, ed. *Female Suicide Terrorists* (Tel Aviv: Jaffe Center for Strategic Studies, 2003), 20–21.

5. Victor, *Army of Roses,* 33–34.

6. For more information on the Hamburg Cell, see Kim Cragin and Scott Gerwehr, *Dissuading Terror: Strategic Influence and the Struggle against Terrorism* (Santa Monica: RAND Corporation, 2005).

7. Ibid.

8. Abdullah Anas, *The Birth of the Afghani Arabs: A Biography of Abdullah Anas with Mas'oud and Abdullah Azzam,* trans. Nadia Masid (London: Dar el-Saqi, 2002).

9. Peter Bergen, "My Brother Osama, How Many Innocent People Have Been Killed?" *The Independent*, 22 June 2008.

10. Robert A. Pape, *Dying to Win: The Strategic Logic of Suicide Terrorism* (New York: Random House, 2006).

11. Stephen Holmes, "Al-Qaeda, 11 September 2001," in *Making Sense of Suicide Missions*, ed. Diego Gambetta (Oxford: Oxford University Press, 2005), 131–73.

12. "The Jemaah Islamiyyah Arrests and the Threat of Terrorism," Singapore Government White Paper, 7 January 2003.

13. Ibid.

14. Marc Sageman, *Understanding Terrorist Networks* (Philadelphia: Pennsylvania University Press, 2004).

15. Anne Speckhard and Khapta Akhmedova, "Black Widows: The Chechen Female Suicide Terrorists," in Schweitzer, *Female Suicide Terrorists*, 63.

16. Ibid.; see also Kim Murphy, "Black Widows Caught Up in Web of Chechen War," *LA Times*, 7 February 2004.

17. Anne Speckhard and Khapta Ahkmedova, "The Making of a Martyr: Chechen Suicide Terrorism," 447.

18. Anne Speckhard and Khapta Akhmedova, "Black Widows: The Chechen Female Suicide Terrorists," in *Female Suicide Terrorists*, 63.

19. Yoram Schweitzer, "Palestinian Female Suicide Bombers: Myths versus Reality," in *Female Suicide Terrorists*, ed. Yoram Schweitzer (Tel Aviv: Jaffe Center for Strategic Studies, 2003). In general, it is difficult to gauge the degree of "successful" suicide bombing attempts in Israel, because Israeli authorities have implemented aggressive preventative measures. That is, some of the women in Schweitzer's study never apparently moved beyond the planning stages of the attack, so it is difficult to determine if they would have carried through with the attack or not. Perhaps arrested suicide bombers, especially those arrested in the planning stages, have different factors motivating them and are not as committed as those who succeeded?

20. For more information on these attacks, see David Rudge, "Female Suicide Bomber Kills Three at Afula Mall," *Jerusalem Post*, 20 May 2003; "Two Palestinians Killed in Gaza, Would-Be Female Bomber Nabbed," Agence France Presse, 20 October 2004; "Did Reem Love Allah More Than Her Children?" *al-Bawaba*, 17 February 2004; "Israelis: Woman Suicide Bomber Caught," UPI, 20 June 2005; "Female Bombmaker Nabbed as Security Forces Smash Hamas Terror Cells," Israel Insider, 11 October 2005; Cameron W. Barr, "Why a Palestinian Girl Now Wants to Be a Suicide Bomber," *Christian Science Monitor*, 1 April 2002, 7; Harry de Quetteville, "Hamas Women's Wing Takes up Weapons 'for the Love of Jihad,'" *Telegraph*, 2 October 2005; Margot Dudkevitch, "Female Suicide Bombers on the Rise," *Jerusalem Post*, 15 January 2004, 3; "Suicide Attack Was 8th by Female," *Jerusalem Post*, 23 September 2004, 3; "Female Bomber Planned to Blow up at Soroka Hospital," *Jerusalem Post*, 21 June 2005, 1.

21. Schweitzer, *Female Suicide Terrorists*, 26.

22. Ibid., 35-36.

23. Alyssa J Rubin, "Despair Drives Suicide Attacks by Iraqi Women," *The New York Times*, June 5, 2008.

24. Alex Kingsbury, "The Rising Number of Female Suicide Bombers in Iraq," *US News and World Report,* 28 July 2008.

25. Craig Smith, "Police Try to Fathom Belgian Path to Terror," *International Herald Tribune,* 6 December 2005.

26. Nicola Smith, "Making of Muriel the Suicide Bomber," *Sunday Times,* 4 December 2005.

27. "Journey of a Belgian Female Suicide Bomber," *BBC News,* 2 December 2005.

28. Bobby Ghosh, "The Mind of a Female Suicide Bomber," *Time Magazine,* 22 June 2008.

29. Pape, *Dying to Win,* 27-61.

30. "Interview with Sheikh Ahmad Yasin," Palestinian Information Center, 17 January 2004, www.palestine-info.net (accessed 28 December 2005).

31. Julian Madsen, "Suicide Terrorism, Rationalizing the Irrational," *Strategic Insights* 3, no. 8 (August 2004).

32. Ehud Sprinzak, "Rational Fanatics," *Foreign Policy,* September/October 2000.

33. Nihat Ali Özcan, "PKK's Recruitment of Female Operatives," *Jamestown Monitor* 4, no. 28 (11 September 2007).

34. Ibid.

35. Ibid.

36. For more information on the women of the LTTE, see the LTTE Web site at http://www.tamilnation.org/women/tamileEelam.htm (accessed 30 November 2007).

37. Ibid.

38. Farhana Ali, "Dressed to Kill," *Newsweek,* 30 July 2008.

39. "The Rise of the Female Suicide Bomber," *Associated Press,* 7 June 2008.

40. Peter Bergen and Paul Cruickshank, "Veiled Threats: Meet the New Face of Terror," *Washington Post,* 12 August 2007.

41. Ibid.

42. "Did Reem Love Allah More Than Her Children?" *al-Bawaba.*

Chapter 5

1. For more information on FARC women fighters, see the FARC Web site at http://www.farc-ep.org (accessed 2 February 2009); see also, Jeremy McDermott, "Colombia's Female Fighting Force," *BBC News,* 4 January 2002, http://www.latinamericanstudies.org/farc/farc-females.htm (accessed 23 October 2007); and "Eliana Gonzalez," *BBC News,* 27 May 2004, http://news.bbc.co.uk/1/shared/spl/hi/programmes/this_world/one_day_of_war/html/12.stm (accessed 22 September 2007).

2. Linda L. Reif, "Women in Latin American Guerrilla Movements: A Comparative Perspective," *Comparative Politics,* 18, no. 2 (January 1986), 147–68.

3. "Triumph of the Sandinistas," *Time,* 4 September 1978.

4. Thomas Sheehan, "Italy: Behind the Ski Mask," *New York Review of Books* 26, no. 13 (16 August 1979).

5. Alison Jamieson, "Mafioso and Terrorists: Italian Women in Violent Organizations," *SAIS Review* 20, no. 2 (Summer/Fall 2000), 51–64.

6. Daniel E. Georges-Abeyie, "Women as Terrorists," in *Perspectives on Terrorism*, ed. Lawrence Freedman and Yonah Alexander (Wilmington: Scholarly Resources, 1983), 73.

7. Rhiannon Talbot, "Myths in the Representation of Women Terrorists," *Eire-Ireland* 35, no. 3-4 (2001), 2.

8. Alan Krueger and Jitka Malekova, "Education, Poverty and Terrorism: Is There a Causal Connection?" *The Journal of Economic Perspectives* 17, no. 4 (Autumn 2003), 119–44.

9. Ibid., 130.

10. Ibid., 130–35.

11. Albert Bandura, "Mechanisms of Moral Disengagement," in *Origins of Terrorism: Psychologies, Ideologies, Theologies, States of Mind,* ed. Walter Reich (Washington, DC: Woodrow Wilson Press, 1998), 161–91.

12. LTTE Web site, www.tamilnation.org (accessed 4 September 2007).

13. Ibid.

14. "Tamil Tigers Mark Anniversary of First Suicide Attack," Agence France Presse, 5 July 2005.

15. LTTE Web site.

16. "Greetings on International Womens' Day," statement posted on FARC Web site, 8 March 2005, and reported in the Colombian press and BBC News. "FARC Statement Praises Role of Colombia's Female Guerrillas," *BBC Worldwide Monitoring*, 14 March 2005, accessed on LexisNexis Academic Universe (accessed 29 December 2005).

17. de la Vega, "Colombia's Tough Rebel Women Fight to the Death," *The Sunday Telegraph*, 16 January 2005, accessed on LexisNexis Academic Universe (accessed 29 December 2005).

18. Rachel Van Dongen, "A Coed's Path from Poli-sci Major to Leftist Guerilla," *Christian Science Monitor*, 10 February 2004, accessed on LexisNexis Academic Universe (accessed 29 December 2005).

19. Ibid.

20. Ibid.

21. de la Vega, "Colombia's Tough Rebel Women Fight to the Death."

22. Ibid.

23. McDermott, "Colombia's Female Fighting Force."

24. Ibid. and "Eliana Gonzalez," *BBC News*.

25. Nathaniel Nash, "Shining Path Women: So Many and So Ferocious," *New York Times*, 22 September 1992.

26. David Scott Palmer, ed., *The Shining Path of Peru*, 2nd ed. (New York: St Martin's Press, 1994), 34.

27. M. Eliana Mar, "The Role of Women in the Shining Path Movement," *Harvard Magazine*, May 1996, http://harvardmagazine.com/1996/05/right.violence.html (accessed 10 October 2006).

28. Hugh O'Shannessey, "Peru's Red Sun of Terror Sets," *The Observer*, 25 July 1993.

29. Deborah Haynes, "The Kurdish Women Rebels Who Are Ready to Fight and Die for Their Cause," *The Times*, 24 October 2007.

30. "Big Successes Still to Come," *Kurdistan Report* #27, November 1998, http://www.etext.org/Politics/Arm.The.Spirit/Kurdistan/PKK.ERNK.ARGK/pkk-cc-interview-1998.txt (accessed 23 October 2008).

31. Jamieson, "Mafiosi and Terrorists: Italian Women in Violent Organizations," 54.

32. Ibid., 56.

33. Ibid., 55.

34. Georges-Abeyie, "Women as Terrorists," 71–84.

35. Talbot, "Myths in the Representation of Women Terrorists," 3.

36. Ibid.

37. Leila Khaled, *My People Shall Live: An Autobiography of a Revolutionary,* ed. George Hajjar (London: Hodder and Stoughton, 1973), 108, 110.

38. "Syrians Release Arab Hijackers," *St. Petersburg Times*, 14 October 1969; Leila Khaled, *My People Shall Live: An Autobiography of a Revolutionary*, 108, 110.

39. "Transcripts: The Guerrilla's Story," *BBC News*, 1 January 2001.

40. "In the Spotlight: Japanese Red Army Faction," Center for Defense Information, http://www.cdi.org/friendlyversion/printversion.cfm?documentID=1771 (accessed 10 April 2008).

41. Rosie Cowan, "I have no regrets," *The Guardian*, 13 March 2003.

42. Ibid.

43. Ibid., see also "Transcripts: The Guerrilla's Story," *BBC News*.

44. "Interview with Leila Khaled in the Guardian—2000," 26 January 2000, http://www.pflp.ps/english/?q=interview-leila-khaled-guardian-2000 (accessed 28 October 2008).

Chapter 6

1. Definition available online at Merriam-Webster Online Dictionary, http://www.merriam-webster.com/dictionary/vanguard (accessed 11 November 2008).

2. Robin Kirk, *The Monkey's Paw: New Chronicles from Peru*, (Thomas-Shore, 1997), 89–91.

3. Ibid.

4. "Rebel Chief Going on Trial," *Miami Herald*, 26 September 2005.

5. Naim Qassam, *Hizballah: The Story from Within* (London: Saqi Books, 2005).

6. Clare Murphy, "Who Were the Baader-Meinhof Gang?" *BBC News*, 12 February 2007, http://news.bbc.co.uk/2/hi/europe/6314559.stm (accessed 2 February 2009).

7. For more information on the Baader-Meinhof group, see www.baader-meinhof.com (accessed 2 February 2009).

8. Eileen MacDonald, *Shoot the Women First* (New York: Random House, 1991), 211.

9. Ibid., 201.

10. Ibid., 209.

11. Ibid.

12. Alison Jamieson, "Mafiosi and Terrorists: Italian Women in Violent Organizations," *SAIS Review* 20, no. 2 (Summer/Fall 2000), 51–64.

13. MacDonald, *Shoot the Women First*, 182.

14. Jamieson, "Mafiosi and Terrorists: Italian Women in Violent Organizations," 58.

15. MacDonald, *Shoot the Women First*, 170.

16. Ibid., 184.

17. Maria Alvanou, "Criminology and the Study of Female Suicide Terrorism," in *Female Suicide Bombers: Dying for Equality?* ed. Yoram Schweitzer (Tel Aviv: Jafee Center for Strategic Studies, August 2005). Memorandum no. 84.

18. MacDonald, *Shoot the Women First*, 184.

19. Ibid., 174.

20. Rhiannon Talbot, "Myths in the Representation of Female Terrorists," *Eire-Ireland* 35, no. 3-4 (2001), 2.

21. Ibid.

22. MacDonald, *Shoot the Women First*, 170.

23. Ibid., 175.

24. Jamieson, "Mafiosi and Terrorists: Italian Women in Violent Organizations," 56.

25. Simon Freeman, "Japan's Female Terror Leader Is Jailed for 20 Years," Times Online, 23 February 2006, http://www.timesonline.co.uk/tol/news/world/asia/article734044.ece (accessed 2 February 2009).

26. Ibid.

27. Japanese Red Army (JRA), Anti-Imperialist International Brigade (AIIB), Federation of American Scientists, http://www.fas.org/irp/world/para/jra.htm (accessed 2 February 2009).

28. Red Army's Reign of Terror, BBC.com, 8 November 2000, http://news.bbc.co.uk/1/hi/world/asia-pacific/1013172.stm (accessed 2 February 2009).

29. Mark Magnier, "Daughters of Red Terrorists Emerge from Expatriate Lives," *The Los Angeles Times*, 3 June 2001, http://amarillo.com/stories/060301/usn_ofred.shtml (accessed 2 February 2009).

30. Mark Schreiber, "My Mother, the Terrorist and Other Successful Families," *The Japan Times*, 10 June 2003, http://search.japantimes.co.jp/cgi-bin/fl20030610zg.html (accessed 2 February 2009).

31. Freeman, "Japan's Female Terror Leader Is Jailed for 20 Years."

32. "Japanese Red Army Leader Jailed," *The Journal of Turkish Weekly*, 23 February 2006, http://www.turkishweekly.net/news.php?id=26427 (accessed 2 February 2009).

33. Freeman, "Japan's Female Terror Leader Is Jailed for 20 Years."

34. "Anadolu Agency: News in English," *HRI Report*, 6 January 1999, http://www.hri.org/news/turkey/anadolu/1999/99-06-01.anadolu.html (accessed 12 November 2008).

35. "Ocalan denies role in key rebel actions," *CNN News,* 1 January 1999, http://www.cnn.com/WORLD/meast/9906/01/ocalan.02/ (accessed 12 November 2008).

36. *Five Letters to the Africa Corps,* September 1993–May 1994, U.S. military document number AFGP-2002-600053, http://cisac.stanford.edu/publications/harmony_and_disharmony_exploiting_alqaidas_organizational_vulnerabilities/ (accessed 2 February 2009).

37. "Comandante Ramona, Zapatista Leader," *Boston Globe,* 8 January 2006, http://www.boston.com/news/globe/obituaries/articles/2006/01/08/comandante_ramona_zapatista_leader (accessed 12 November 2008).

38. "Message from Comandante Ramona to Students at University City," http://flag.blackened.net/revolt/mexico/ezln/1997/romana_at_uni_mar.html (accessed 12 November 2008).

39. Kevin Cullen, "Hunger Striker's Kin Sees Ulster Sellout," *Boston Globe,* 19 May 1998.

40. "Bobby Sands' Sister Speaks Out," *Marxism,* 3 August 2005, http://archives.econ.utah.edu/archives/marxism/2005w31/msg00162.htm (accessed 12 November 2008).

41. "ETA Women Emerge as Top Guns in Terror War," *The Observer,* 24 September 2000, http://www.guardian.co.uk/world/2000/sep/24/spain.theobserver (accessed 8 November 2008).

42. Hala Bonpamcagni, "Hizballah Picks First Woman for Top Post," *Dawn,* 15 May 2005, http://www.dawn.com/2005/05/15/int18.htm (accessed 13 November 2008).

43. Dina Abdel Mageed, "A Leading Woman Member of Hizballah," *Islam Online,* 18 May 2006, http://www.islamonline.net/English/Views/2006/05/article03.shtml (accessed 13 November 2008).

44. Fatima el-Issawi, "Hizballah: Mothers of Martyrs," *Ashraq al-Awsat,* 8 December 2007, http://www.asharqalawsat.com/english/news.asp?section=3&id=9864 (accessed 13 November 2008).

45. Results of Public Opinion Polls, An Najah National University, 5-6 January 2006, http://www.najah.edu/english/news/show.asp?key=252 (accessed 20 February 2006).

46. "Sinn Fein: Delivering for Ireland's Future," *Sinn Fein Manifesto,* 2007, http://cain.ulst.ac.uk/issues/politics/election/manifestos.htm (accessed 13 November 2008).

Chapter 7

1. "US Trains Iraqi Women to Find Female Suicide Bombers," *CNN News,* 24 June 2008, http://www.cnn.com/2008/WORLD/meast/06/24/daughters.of.iraq/index.html (accessed 1 November 2008).

2. Lawrence Wright, "The Rebellion Within: An Al-Qaeda Mastermind Questions Terrorism," *The New Yorker,* 2 June 2008.

Bibliography

"22-year-old woman accused of making Hamas bombs." *USA Today*, 11 October 2005. www.usatoday.com/news/world/2005-10-11-hamasbombs_x.htm.

Ali, Farhana. "Ready to Detonate: The Diverse Profiles of Female Suicide Bombers." *The MIPT Terrorism Annual*, November 2006.

———. "Dressed to Kill." *Newsweek*, 30 July 2008.

Alison, Miranda. "Women as Agents of Political Violence: Gendering Security." *Security Dialogue* 35 (2004).

"Al-Qaeda Faces Gender Debate." CNN.com, 1 June 2008. http://www.cnn.com/2008/WORLD/meast/06/01/alqaeda.women.ap/index.html.

"Al-Qaeda's Women's Magazine: Women Must Participate in Jihad." Special Dispatch Series no. 779, 7 September 2004. http://memri.org/bin/articles.cgi?Page=archives&Area=sd&ID=SP77904#_edn1.

Alvanou, Maria. "Criminology and the Study of Female Suicide Terrorism." In *Female Suicide Bombers: Dying for Equality?* edited by Yoram Schweitzer, Tel Aviv: Jafee Center for Strategic Studies. Memorandum no. 84, 2006.

"Al-Zawahiri: No Women in Al-Qa'ida Ranks." *CBS News*, 22 April 2008. http://www.cbsnews.com/stories/2008/04/22/cbsnews_investigates/main4033865.shtml (accessed 10 October 2008).

Anas, Abdullah. *The Birth of the Afghani Arabs: A Biography of Abdullah Anas with Mas'oud and Abdullah Azzam*, trans. Nadia Masid. London: Dar el-Saqi, 2002.

Background Paper on Female Suicide Terrorism: Consequences for Counterterrorism, OSCE Technical Workshop on Suicide Terrorism, Warsaw, Poland, 20 May 2005. http://www.osce.org/documents/odihr/2005/05/14827_en.pdf.

Bakker, Edwin. *Jihadists in Europe—Their Characteristics and the Circumstances in which They Joined the Jihad: An Exploratory Study*. Clingendael: Netherlands Institute of International Relations, 2006.

Barr, Cameron W. "Why a Palestinian Girl Now Wants to be a Suicide Bomber." *Christian Science Monitor,* 1 April 2002. http://www.csmonitor.com/2002/0401/p07s01-wome.html.

Behn, Sharon. "Female Bombers Spreading More Terror." *The Washington Times,* 20 March 2008. http://www.washingtontimes.com/apps/pbcs.dll/article?AID=/20080320/FOREIGN/373394613.

Bell, J. Bowyer, *The IRA, 1968–2000: Analysis of a Secret Army.* London: Frank Cass, 2000.

Berko, Anat, and Edna Erez. "Gender, Palestinian Women, and Terrorism: Women's Liberation or Oppression?" *Studies in Conflict and Terrorism* 30, no. 6 (1 June 2007).

Bergen, Peter, and Paul Cruickshank. "Veiled Threats: Meet the New Face of Terror." *Washington Post,* 12 August 2007.

Bergen, Peter. "My Brother Osama, How Many Innocent People Have Been Killed?" *The Independent,* 22 June 2008.

"Big Successes Still to Come." *Kurdistan Report* #27, November 1998. http://www.etext.org/Politics/Arm.The.Spirit/Kurdistan/PKK.ERNK.ARGK/pkk-cc-interview-1998.txt. (accessed 23 October 2008).

Bloom, Mia. "Female suicide bombers: a global trend." *Daedalus* 136, no. 1 (Winter 2007).

————. "Mother, Daughter, Sister, Bomber." *Bulletin of the Atomic Scientists,* November/December 2005.

"Bobby Sands' Sister Speaks Out." *Marxism,* 3 August 2005. http://archives.econ.utah.edu/archives/marxism/2005w31/msg00162.htm (accessed 12 November 2008).

Bonpamcagni, Hala. "Hizballah Picks First Woman for Top Post." *Dawn,* 15 May 2005. http://www.dawn.com/2005/05/15/int18.htm (accessed 13 November 2008).

Caiazza, Amy. "Why Gender Matters in Understanding September 11: Women, Militarism, and Violence." Briefing Paper, Institute for Women's Policy Research, November 2001. http://www.iwpr.org/pdf/terrorism.pdf.

"CIA Helps Defuse al-Qaeda Bomb Plot in Morocco." CNN News, 16 June 2002. http://archives.cnn.com/2002/WORLD/africa/06/16/terror.arrests/index.html (accessed 10 October 2008).

"Comandante Ramona, Zapatista Leader." *Boston Globe,* 8 January 2006. http://www.boston.com/news/globe/obituaries/articles/2006/01/08/comandante_ramona_zapatista_leader/ (accessed 12 November 2008).

Cook, David. "Women Fighting in Jihad?" *Studies in Conflict and Terrorism* 28, (2005): 375–84.

Cowan, Rosie. "'I have no regrets.'" *The Guardian,* 13 March 2003.

Cragin, Kim, and Scott Gerwehr. *Dissuading Terror: Strategic Influence and the Struggle against Terrorism.* Santa Monica: RAND Corporation, 2005.

Cunningham, Karla. "Countering Female Terrorism." *Studies in Conflict and Terrorism* 30, no. 2 (1 February 2007).

————. "Cross-Regional Trends in Female Terrorism." *Studies in Conflict and Terrorism* 26, no. 3 (1 May 2003).

Daniel, Naila. "Palestinian Women in the Intifada." *Peace Magazine* 13, no. 4 (July-August 1997).

Damon, Arwa. "Iraqi Woman Describes Daughter's Descent into Suicide Bombing." CNN.com, 6 June 2008. http://edition.cnn.com/2008/WORLD/meast/06/06/female.bombers/index.html.

de la Vega, Elena. "Colombia's Tough Rebel Women Fight to the Death." *The Sunday Telegraph*, 16 January 2005.

de Quetteville, Harry. "Hamas Women's Wing Takes Up Weapons 'for the Love of Jihad.'" *UK Telegraph*, 2 October 2005.

Dickey, Christopher. "Women of al-Qaeda." *Newsweek*, 12 December 2005.

"Did Reem Love Allah More than Her Children?" *al-Bawaba*, 17 February 2004.

Dudkevitch, Margot. "Female Suicide Bombers on the Rise." *Jerusalem Post*, 15 January 2004.

———. "Suicide Attack Was 8th by Female." *Jerusalem Post*, 23 September 2004.

———. "Female Bomber Planned to Blow Up at Soroka Hospital." *Jerusalem Post*, 21 June 2005.

Eager, Paige Whaley. *From Freedom Fighters to Terrorists: Women and Political Violence*. New York: Ashgate Publishing, 2008.

"Eliana Gonzalez." BBC News, 27 May 2004. http://news.bbc.co.uk/1/shared/spl/hi/programmes/this_world/one_day_of_war/html/12.stm.

Emerson, Steven. *American Jihad: The Terrorists Living Among Us*. New York: Free Press, 2002.

"ETA women emerge as top guns in terror war." *The Observer*, 24 September 2000. http://www.guardian.co.uk/world/2000/sep/24/spain.theobserver (accessed 8 November 2008).

Fairweather, Eileen, et al. *Only the Rivers Run Free: Northern Ireland: The Women's War*. London: Pluto Press, 1984.

"FARC Statement Praises Role of Colombia's Female Guerrillas." *BBC Worldwide Monitoring*, 14 March 2005.

"FBI Terrorism Swoop." BBC News, 30 December 1999. http://news.bbc.co.uk/1/hi/world/americas/584144.stm (accessed 30 October 2007).

"Female Bombmaker Nabbed as Security Forces Smash Hamas Terror Cells." *Israel Insider*, 11 October 2005.

Finn, Peter. "Al-Qaeda Deputies Harbored by Iran." *Washington Post*, 28 August 2002, A01.

Five Letters to the Africa Corps, September 1993–May 1994, U.S. military document number AFGP-2002-600053. http://cisac.stanford.edu/publications/harmony_and_disharmony__exploiting_alqaidas_organizational_vulnerabilities/.

Foden, Giles. "Death and the Maidens." *The Guardian*, 18 July 2003.

Freedman, Lawrence Zelic, and Yonah Alexander, eds. *Perspectives on Terrorism*. Wilmington: Scholarly Resources, 1983.

Freeman, Simon. "Japan's Female Terror Leader Is Jailed for 20 Years." *Times Online*, 23 February 2006. http://www.timesonline.co.uk/tol/news/world/asia/article734044.ece.

Gambetta, Diego, ed. *Making Sense of Suicide Missions*. Oxford: Oxford University Press, 2005.

Ghosh, Bobby. "The Mind of a Female Suicide Bomber." *Time,* 22 June 2008.

Gorriti, Gustavo. *The Shining Path: A History of the Millenarian War in Peru,* Robin Kirk, trans. Chapel Hill, NC: University of North Carolina Press, 1999.

Gottlieb, Sebastiaan. "A Dutch Woman's FARC Diaries." Radio Netherlands Worldwide, 9 April 2007. http://www.radionetherlands.nl/currentaffairs/ ned070904mc#diary.

Haas, Amira. *Drinking the Sea at Gaza: Days and Nights in a Land Under Seige.* New York: Henry Holt and Company, 1999.

Hafez, Mohammed. "Manufacturing Human Bombs: Strategy, Culture, and Conflict in the Making of Palestinian Suicide Bombers." United States Institute of Peace, 4 April 2005. http://www.utexas.edu/cola/depts/government/ content/events/workshop_papers/hafez.pdf.

"Hamas Spokesman Praises Palestinian Grandmother Suicide Bomber, Calls for Attacks in the Heart of Israel." Special Dispatch Series no. 1383, The Middle East Media Research Institute, 7 December 2006. http://memri.org/ bin/articles.cgi?Page=archives&Area=sd&ID=SP138306.

Hammimi, Rema. "Women, the Hijab and the Uprising." *Middle East Report,* May/August 1990, 24–28.

Haynes, Deborah. "The Kurdish Women Rebels Who Are Ready to Fight and Die for Their Cause." *The Times,* 24 October 2007.

Hermann, Peter. "Lining Up to Die." *Baltimore Sun,* 31 January 2004.

Hilterman, Joost. "Trade Unions and Women's Committees: Sustaining Movement, Creating Space." *Middle East Report,* May/August 1990, 32–36.

Hyun Hee, Kim. *The Tears of My Soul.* New York: William Morrow and Company, 1993.

"Israelis: Woman Suicide Bomber Caught." UPI, 20 June 2005.

el-Issawi, Fatima. "Hizballah: Mothers of Martyrs." *Ashraq al-Awsat,* 8 December 2007. http://www.asharqalawsat.com/english/news.asp?section=3&id=9864 (accessed 13 November 2008).

Jacinto, Leela. "Al-Qaeda's 'Female Squads' Go Online." ABC News.com, 23 September 2004. http://abcnews.go.com/International/story?id=84585& page=1.

Jamieson, Alison. "Mafiosi and Terrorists: Italian Women in Violent Organizations." *SAIS Review* 20, no. 2 (Summer/Fall): 51–64.

"Japanese Red Army (JRA), Anti-Imperialist International Brigade (AIIB)." Federation of American Scientists. http://www.fas.org/irp/world/para/jra. htm.

"Japanese Red Army Leader Jailed." *Journal of Turkish Weekly,* 23 February 2006. http://www.turkishweekly.net/news.php?id=26427.

"The Jemaah Islamiyyah Arrests and the Threat of Terrorism." Singapore Government White Paper, 7 January 2003.

"Jemaah Islamiyyah: Damaged but Still Dangerous." *Asia Report No. 63,* August 2003.

Jordan, Kim, and Miram Denov. "Birds of Freedom? Perspectives on Female Emancipation and the Liberation Tigers of Tamil Eelam." *Journal of International Women's Studies* 9, no. 1 (November 2007): 52.

Khaled, Leila. *My People Shall Live.* George Hajjar, ed. London: Hodder and Stoughton, 1973.

Kingsbury, Alex. "The Rising Number of Female Suicide Bombers in Iraq." *US News and World Report,* 28 July 2008.

Kirk, Robin. *The Monkey's Paw: New Chronicles from Peru.* Amherst, MA: University of Massachusetts Press, 1997.

Koons, Jennifer. "Al-Qaeda in Iraq—Down But Not Out." *Iraqi Crisis Report No. 266,* 25 July 2008. http://www.iwpr.net/index.php?apc_state=hen&s=o&o=l=EN&p=icr&s=f&o=345878 (accessed 10 October 2008).

Krueger, Alan, and Jitka Malekova. "Education, Poverty and Terrorism: Is there a Causal Connection?" *Journal of Economic Perspectives* 17, no. 4 (Autumn 2003): 119–44.

MacDonald, Eileen. *Shoot the Women First.* New York: Random House, 1991.

Madsen, Julian. "Suicide Terrorism, Rationalizing the Irrational." *Strategic Insights* 3, no. 8 (August 2004).

Mageed, Dina Abdel. "A Leading Woman Member of Hizballah." *Islam Online,* 18 May 2006. http://www.islamonline.net/English/Views/2006/05/article03.shtml (accessed 13 November 2008).

Magnier, Mark. "Daughters of Red Terrorists Emerge from Expatriate Lives." *The Los Angeles Times,* 3 June 2001. http://amarillo.com/stories/060301/usn_ofred.shtml.

Maqdsi, Mohammad, trans. "The Charter of the Islamic Resistance Movement." *Journal of Palestine Studies* 22 (Spring 1993): 122–34.

Mar, Eliana M. "The Role of Women in the Shining Path Movement." *Harvard Magazine,* May 1996. http://harvardmagazine.com/1996/05/right.violence.html (accessed 10 October 2006).

"Mauritanian Police Say Mastermind behind the Christmas Eve Killings of French Tourists Arrested." Associated Press, 10 April 2008. http://www.iht.com/articles/ap/2008/04/10/africa/AF-GEN-Mauritania-Tourist-Killings.php (accessed 10 October 2008).

McDermott, Jeremy. "Colombia's Female Fighting Force." BBC News, 4 January 2002. http://www.latinamericanstudies.org/farc/farc-females.htm.

McGirk, Tim. "Palestinian Moms Becoming Martyrs." TIME.com, 3 May 2007. http://www.time.com/time/magazine/article/0,9171,1617542,00.html.

McGeary, Johanna. "New Year's Evil." *Time,* 26 December 1999. http://www.time.com/time/magazine/article/0,9171,36512-1,00.html (accessed 23 June 2007).

"Message from Comandante Ramona to Students at University City." http://flag.blackened.net/revolt/mexico/ezln/1997/romana_at_uni_mar.html (accessed 12 November 2008).

Mishal, Shaul, and Reuben Aharoni. *Speaking Stones: Communiqués from the Intifada Underground.* New York: Syracuse University Press, 1994.

Morgan, Valerie. "Peacemakers? Peacekeepers? Women in Northern Ireland 1969–1995." A Professorial Lecture Given at the University of Ulster, 25 October 1995. http://cain.ulst.ac.uk/issues/women/paper3.htm.

"Morocco Uncovers al-Qaeda Plot." BBC News, 11 June 2002. http://news.bbc.co.uk/2/hi/africa/2037391.stm (accessed 10 October 2008).

Murphy, Clare. "Who were the Baader-Meinhof Gang?" BBC News, 12 February 2007. http://news.bbc.co.uk/2/hi/europe/6314559.stm.

Murphy, Kim. "Black Widows Caught Up in Web of Chechen War." *LA Times,* 7 February 2004.

Myers, Steven Lee. "From Dismal Chechnya, Women Turn to Bombs." *New York Times,* 10 September 2004.

Nacos, Bridget. "The Portrayal of Female Terrorists in the Media: Similar Framing Patterns in the News Coverage of Women in Politics and Terrorism." *Studies in Conflict and Terrorism* 28, no. 5 (September-October 2005).

Nash, Nathanial C.. "Lima Journal: Shining Path Women: So Many and So Ferocious." *The New York Times,* 22 September 1992.

Ness, Cindy D. "In the Name of the Cause: Women's Work in Secular and Religious Terrorism." *Studies in Conflict and Terrorism* 28, 2005.

Novikov, Evgenii. "The Recruiting and Organizational Structure of Hizb ut-Tahrir." *Terrorism Monitor* 2(22), The Jamestown Foundation, 18 November 2004. http://www.jamestown.org/publications_details.php?volume_id=400&issue_id=3148&article_id=2368890.

"Ocalan Denies Role in Key Rebel Actions." CNN News, 1 June 1999. http://www.cnn.com/WORLD/meast/9906/01/ocalan.02/ (accessed 12 November 2008).

O'Connor, Alisa Stack. "Lions, Tigers, and Freedom Birds: How and Why the Liberation Tigers of Tamil Eelam Employs Women." *Terrorism and Political Violence* 19 (2007).

O'Shannessey, Hugh. "Peru's Red Sun of Terror Sets." *The Observer,* 25 July 1993.

Özcan, Nihat Ali. "PKK's Recruitment of Female Operatives." *Jamestown Monitor* 4, no. 28 (11 September 2007).

"Palestinian MP From Hamas Dr. Yunis al-Astal on Women's Participation in Jihad—From Islam's Beginnings to Modern Female Suicide Bombers." Special Dispatch Series no. 1631, The Middle East Media Research Institute, 22 July 2007. http://memri.org/bin/articles.cgi?Page=archives&Area=sd&ID=SP163107.

"Palestinian 'Targeted Hospital,'" BBC News, 21 June 2005. http://news.bbc.co.uk/2/hi/middle_east/4113538.stm (accessed 3 November 2008).

Palmer, David Scott, ed. *The Shining Path of Peru.* 2nd ed. New York: St. Martin's Press, 1994.

Pape, Robert A. *Dying to Win: The Strategic Logic of Suicide Terrorism.* New York: Random House, 2006.

Patkin, Terri Toles. "Explosive Baggage: Female Palestinian Suicide Bombers and the Rhetoric of Emotion." *HighBeam Research,* July 18, 2005. www.highbeam.com/doc/1G1-130469595.html (accessed 28 December 2005).

Qassam, Naim. *Hizballah: The Story from Within.* London: Saqi Books, 2005.

"Rebel Chief Going on Trial." *Miami Herald,* 26 September 2005.

"Red Army's Reign of Terror." CNN.com, 8 November 2000. http://news.bbc.co.uk/1/hi/world/asia-pacific/1013172.stm.

Reich, Walter, ed. *Origins of Terrorism: Psychologies, Ideologies, Theologies, States of Mind.* Washington, D.C.: Woodrow Wilson Press, 1998.

Reif, Linda L. "Women in Latin American Guerrilla Movements: A Comparative Perspective." *Comparative Politics* 18, no. 2 (January 1986): 147–68.

"Report no. 2000/04: International Terrorism: The Threat to Canada." Canadian Security Intelligence Service, 3 May 2000. http://www.csis-scrs.gc.ca/pblctns/prspctvs/200004-eng.asp.

"Results of Public Opinion Polls." An Najah National University. 5-6 January 2006. http://www.najah.edu/english/news/show.asp?key=252 (accessed 20 February 2006).

Rubin, Alyssa J. "Despair Drives Suicide Attacks by Iraqi Women." *The New York Times,* June 5, 2008.

Rudge, David. "Female Suicide Bomber Kills Three at Afula Mall." *Jerusalem Post,* 20 May 2003.

Sageman, Marc. *Understanding Terrorist Networks*: Philadelphia: Pennsylvania University Press, 2004.

Schreiber, Mark. "My Mother, the Terrorist and Other Successful Families." *The Japan Times,* 10 June 2003. http://search.japantimes.co.jp/cgi-bin/fl200 30610zg.html.

Schweitzer, Yoram, ed. *Female Suicide Terrorists,* Tel Aviv, Jaffe Center for Strategic Studies, 2006.

Sciolino, Elaine, and Mekhennet Souad. "Belgian Woman Wages War for Al-Qaeda on the Web." *The International Herald Tribune,* 27 May 2008.

Sheehan, Thomas. "Italy: Behind the Ski Mask." *New York Review of Books* 26, no. 13 (16 August 1979).

"Sinn Fein: Delivering for Ireland's Future." *Sinn Fein Manifesto*, 2007. http://cain.ulst.ac.uk/issues/politics/election/manifestos.htm (accessed 13 November 2008).

Smith, Craig. "Police Try to Fathom Belgian Path to Terror." *International Herald Tribune,* 6 December 2005.

Speckhard, Anne, and Khapta Ahkmedova. "The Making of a Martyr: Chechen Suicide Terrorism." *Studies in Conflict and Terrorism* 29, no. 5 (June 2006).

Sprinzak, Ehud. "Rational Fanatics." *Foreign Policy*, September/October 2000.

Stern, Jessica, *Terror in the Name of God: Why Religious Militants Kill.* New York: Harper Collins, 2003.

"Suicide Bomber's Widow Soldiers on." CNN.com, 24 August 2006. http://edition.cnn.com/2006/WORLD/asiapcf/08/15/elaroud/index.html (accessed 5 November 2008).

"Syrians Release Arab Hijackers." *St. Petersburg Times,* 14 October 1969.

Talbot, Rhiannon. "Myths in the Representation of Female Terrorists." *Eire-Ireland*, Fall 2001.

"Tamil Tigers Mark Anniversary of First Suicide Attack." *Agence France Presse,* 5 July 2005.

Torres, Marianne. "Women in the Intifada." *Palestine Papers*, August 1989.

"Transcripts: The Guerrilla's Story." BBC News, 1 January 2001.

"Treasury Designates Members of Abu Ghadiyah's Network Facilitates Flow of Terrorists, Weapons, and Money from Syria to al Qaida in Iraq." Press release, 28 February 2008. http://www.ustreas.gov/press/releases/hp845. htm (accessed 20 October 2008).

"Triumph of the Sandinistas." *Time*, 4 September 1978.

"Two Palestinians Killed in Gaza, Would-Be Female Bomber Nabbed." *Agence France Presse*, 20 October 2004. http://findarticles.com/p/articles/mi_kmafp/is_200410/ai_n8597718.

Van Dongen, Rachel. "A Coed's Path from Poli-sci Major to Leftist Guerilla." *Christian Science Monitor*, 10 February 2004. Accessed on LexisNexis Academic Universe (accessed 29 December 2005).

Victor, Barbara. *Army of Roses: Inside the World of Palestinian Women Suicide Bombers*. New York: Rodale, 2003.

von Knop, Katharina. "The Female Jihad: Al-Qaeda's Women." *Studies in Conflict and Terrorism* 30 (2007).

"Women Tiger Rebels Shot in Sri Lanka After Prince Charles Visit." *Agence France Presse*, 28 February 2005.

Wright, Lawrence. "The Rebellion Within: An Al-Qaeda Mastermind Questions Terrorism." *The New Yorker*, 2 June 2008.

"You'll Learn Not to Cry: Child Combatants in Colombia." *Human Rights Watch Report*. New York: Human Rights Watch, September 2003.

Index

About the Author

R. Kim Cragin, Ph.D., is a senior policy analyst at the RAND Corporation. She focuses on terrorism and has conducted fieldwork in the West Bank and Gaza Strip, Lebanon, Egypt, Colombia, Northern Ireland, Northwest China, Sri Lanka, Southern Thailand, Indonesia, Malaysia, and the Philippines. She is the coauthor of *Dissuading Terror: Strategic Influence and the Struggle Against Terrorism*, *Terrorism and Development*, and *Arms Trafficking and Colombia*.

Sara A. Daly is a lecturer at the George Bush School of Government and Public Service at Texas A&M University. Prior to joining the Bush School, Daly was an international policy analyst at the RAND Corporation, where she coauthored publications on terrorism. She also served as an intelligence analyst at the CIA, specializing in terrorism.